C000227998

THE PERSU

THE
PERSUADER

How To Use Emotional Persuasion
To Win More Business

MARCUS CORAH

bookshaker

First Published In Great Britain 2012
by www.BookShaker.com

© Copyright Marcus Corah

PRAISE FOR THIS BOOK

I am forever looking for new approaches to add to my pitch repertoire. *The Persuader* provides a fantastic summation of what can often be deemed as unconventional. These three magic letters, NLP, cut to the core of what pitching (and good business) is all about. Influencing people.

Melanie Portelli

New Business Director, Saatchi & Saatchi

Marcus has produced a terrific piece of work. This is a great 'how to' book which gives tremendous value if you want to increase your influence in business by understanding your stakeholders' hot buttons. *The Persuader* will help you understand your own emotions better, making you more resilient in managing difficult people and situations.

Romilla Ready

Co-Author of *Neuro-linguistic Programming for Dummies®* – a top selling 'for Dummies®' book which has sold 100,000+ copies worldwide and been translated into 10 languages and *Neuro-linguistic Programming Workbook for Dummies®*

Whatever we are buying, we all buy on the basis of emotion. This practical book explores this fact to help you with your daily client relationships and at pitch critical times. Read it well as the secrets for success lie within.

Liz Nottingham
HR Director, StarCom MediaVest Group

No matter what you are selling, we are all eager to be successful in our sales drive, this however can be challenging in today's economic climate. This most practical and hands-on book will give you useful insights into what triggers your customer to buy and more importantly, to buy from YOU!

Carola van der Linden
Manager, Market Management Public Sector Europe,
Cisco Systems

I have worked with Marcus extensively over the years, introducing him to many of my clients. His knowledge, condensed into this highly readable and practical book, will enable anyone, from any background, to gain the tools necessary to quickly ramp up their effectiveness and their sales success rate. All you have to do is read it, practise it and watch the results speak for themselves!

Avril Millar
Managing Partner of Leadout and The Altitude Club,
executive performance coach

Marcus Corah has put together a clear, concise and useful book that any people in the world of sales and NLP would be wise to have on their shelves. In an industry that so often succumbs to pseudo-science and needlessly confusing jargon, it's refreshing to find a book which is effortlessly readable, whilst being useful and information packed. Personal stories combined with real life examples and straight forward instruction, make the strategies and processes easy for anyone to understand and apply. Use the strategies in this book and follow the advice, and you'll be able to achieve great benefits both in your professional and personal life.

Nathan Thomas

Hypnosis trainer and author of *Keys to the Mind,*
Learn How to Hypnotize Anyone and Practice
Hypnosis and Hypnotherapy Correctly
www.KeysToTheMind.com

ACKNOWLEDGEMENTS

IT'S TRUE; YOU CAN SEE a lot further when you stand on the shoulders of giants. There are so many people who have contributed to the field of NLP, that to single out a few, would undermine the contribution made by so many. So to everyone who has helped me to get to where I am today, thank you.

Having said that, it would be remiss of me not to mention the two co-founders of NLP, Richard Bandler and John Grinder, without whom this field wouldn't exist.

I would also like to thank Rintu Basu, for re-framing some beliefs I had during a lunch a few years ago, so that I actually put pen to paper, or fingers to keys as it is now. His support and encouragement helped to produce the book you're about to read. He's been a source of inspiration and encouragement.

I would like to thank my wife, Rachel, for her continued support while I wrote this book and for helping to shape its content in a way that has undoubtedly made it more digestible.

Finally, Joe and Lucy for agreeing to publish my first book, which hopefully will not be my last, and for all their support and understanding when dealing with someone who has never done this before.

FOREWORD

THIS IS A GREAT BOOK, BUT it is not why I agreed to write
the foreword. I count Marcus as a friend and although
he says good things about me, it is not what compelled
me to write this. In this book you will find many
powerful techniques, insightful perspectives and useful
concepts that I guarantee will dramatically improve
your pitch presentations. But even that is not why I
was keen to write the foreword.

All trainers want a room full of attentive students
eagerly hanging on your every word and desperate to
learn from you. In fact Marcus gives you several ways
of creating this in your audience even when they are
only there for a sales pitch. But good presenters want
even more. They want an audience that will leave the
classroom and do something meaningful. Marcus
shows you how you can move your audience to a call to
action whether that is to sign up, buy now or anything
else you need them to do.

There is one situation that every trainer lives for.
Every now and again someone studies your material;
they apply it to their world, study other ideas and build
that into the mix. Through this they create something
incredible. Marcus has studied really hard, and not just
my material but people that are truly great. He has
added his ideas, his experience and then applied it to

the context of pitch presentations. The result is the book that you hold in your hands and it is truly incredible.

As a trainer there is only one higher accolade that you can give me that is better than using my material to do something great, and that is showing others how to do the same.

I am compelled to write this foreword because I know that if you follow the advice in this book you will automatically become a better presenter and will gain more business. This tool kit can give you serious results. Marcus has done the work for you, he has tested everything and he has created the process so you can pick this book up and run with it and that is why I am really compelled to write this foreword.

Rintu Basu,
Author, *Persuasion Skills Black Book*
www.thenlpcompany.com

CONTENTS

Part Three
Advanced pitch strategies

INTRODUCTION

WELCOME. I HAVEN'T COME ACROSS a better way to introduce myself. It's also how I want you to feel: welcome. And that's what this book is about, connecting emotionally with your clients. Companies know how to engage with their clients logically in a pitch, but how many companies really understand how to engage their clients emotionally as well?

You see, logic doesn't guarantee success. Clients may completely understand all of the logical reasons for hiring you, but they still hire someone else. Why? Because there's a difference between understanding something logically and committing to it emotionally. In your pitch, you want commitment, rather than just understanding.

This book is filled with ideas and techniques that will help you to understand, engage with and manage your clients' emotions during your pitch process. This builds commitment to you, your product or service, your solution and your company.

Here are just a few things you'll discover in this book:

Part One – Maximising your pre-pitch meetings.
- How to build a powerful bond of trust with your clients in your written documents, emails and meetings.

- The questions you must ask to influence your clients' logical decisions in your favour.
- How to identify and neutralise unhelpful beliefs held by your client and capitalise on the helpful ones.
- How to elicit the one thing that will motivate your clients to do what you want.

Part Two – Designing emotionally persuasive content.
- Which emotional states are most likely to create pitch success.
- How to structure your content to increase your persuasiveness.
- How to keep clients engaged during your pitch using emotional hooks.

Part Three – Advanced pitch strategies.
- How to use emotionally persuasive language during your pitch.
- How to use metaphors to reduce resistance to your ideas, resolve problems and elicit emotional states from your clients.
- How to get more of the questions you want at the end of the pitch, and how to answer the tough ones without annoying or frustrating your client.
- And much, much more.

I wanted to bring together the very best information on emotional persuasion and make it available to you in one book. To this end, in addition to my own knowledge, I have referenced some of the world's leading experts on persuasion, NLP and conversational hypnosis.

To get the most from this book, I'm going to recommend you start by applying the ideas that are most useful to you. Don't try to apply lots of these techniques in your next pitch. Building skills is the best way to apply new information.

I won't be there when you make your killer pitch. It won't be me standing over your shoulder that makes it go so well. It will be you, doing it yourself, being brilliant or confident or commanding or persuasive or whatever you need to do to be outstanding. And when you sit down again and you realise what you've just done, how do you think you'll feel? Really think about it for a moment, because what you're feeling comes from building and honing your skills.

I've spent years and tens of thousands of pounds learning and crafting my skills, so that you don't have to. This book is your shortcut, your way to get all of the best knowledge I possess to help you to be more successful.

This means that you're about to learn some very advanced skills. Some people might think these skills are manipulative and, yes, to be honest, you could use this information to manipulate your clients, if that's your aim. Let me tell you what I think manipulation is. It's using these skills to win a client you know you can't service properly, or taking advantage of someone, just because you can. But, if you use these skills and ideas to help your clients succeed, to strengthen a relationship, or to help them believe in themselves, then, to me, that's creating a win-win for both sides. The more you help people succeed, the more, I believe, you succeed too.

Like everything, it's up to you how you use this information, and it's up to you how you work through this book. However, to get the most from it, I'm going to suggest that you read it in order. There's a reason for this. As with your skills, the content builds upon itself, step by step, to build your skills. Skipping ahead might mean that you miss out on how to apply ideas or techniques that have been covered in previous chapters. You will also notice, that I have included exercises for you to do. They are there to help you improve, to help you to be more successful. If you don't start applying the information you've learnt, you won't change your results.

Finally, I have made some assumptions about you, your company and your product or service. I've assumed that you have a great product or service, which will benefit your clients. I have also assumed that, all things being equal, you will win on the strength of your solution, your ability to communicate your solution well and your ability to build a strong emotional bond with your clients. This means that your success rests in your hands. I can't guarantee your results because there are too many variables beyond my control. So, for the purposes of this book, I'm saying that if you apply the ideas you're about to read, I believe you will greatly improve your chances of winning.

So let's start.

OPENING THE LOOP

IT WAS ALMOST FIVE YEARS ago to the month that my life changed. I had gone with my family, to stay with my parents for the weekend. They lived in a beautiful little cottage in the middle of a wheat field. There was nothing between us and the sea apart from the wheat, which, as it was summer time, was ready for harvesting. I love the sea, and I used to walk with my children through the tracks in the field, down to the seawall, where we would scramble up the bank and onto the seawall. When you sit on the seawall, it's like there are so many opportunities, you can see so many adventures unfolding in front of you, you can go anywhere, do anything. It's a great place to think, to let your thoughts drift. Anyway, it was on this particular weekend that everything changed. Because I had taken my family home, my mum decided to have a tea party to introduce us to some other families, who were also up for the weekend. That Saturday afternoon two couples arrived for tea, I knew one of the couples, but not the other. After some pleasantries, I found myself talking to the husband I didn't know. I can't remember his name now, but we started talking, looking for common ground, and I asked him what he did. It turned out he was an architect working in the Far East. At that time I was a director, as in "lights, camera, action" and I was working with an architect who did a few projects in the Far East. Once I said I was a director, he wanted to know the kinds of things I was doing. I told him that I did commercials and high-end corporates. He said it sounded like a great job. I took a moment. I hadn't really thought that much about it before and I certainly hadn't said it out loud, but it wasn't. He looked at me.

"Really," he said. "Why?"

I'm not sure exactly what happened next to make me say what I did; it might have been the sea air or it could have been the fact that I didn't know this person at all, but I felt I could tell him what I really thought. So I just started talking and in that moment, I realised that I wasn't happy with where I was in my life. I wasn't producing the results I wanted to produce. In fact, I felt like a failure. It was a pretty hard thing to admit but deep down I knew it was true. I had failed. And I had said it. Then I realised just how stuck I really was, because when you get into a spiral like that, it's not easy to see a way out. The more you look for answers, the more you realise you don't have any. My stomach knotted the more I thought about it. At some point I remember looking up, into the face of the architect. He stood there with an expression that said "I'm not a therapist and we're at a tea party'.

"Oh God, I'm so sorry, this really isn't anything to do with you. Really, I'm sorry..." He looked at me, smiled and asked,

"If you're not producing the results you want, what are you going to do about it?"

It was a pretty straightforward question, but my mind went completely blank...nothing...silence...it seemed to last for ages...then three letters popped into my head. NLP. I had started to read a book on NLP, got about half-way through and stopped, because 90% of the half I had read made no sense at all. But I knew that was the answer. So I told him, how a friend of mine had met this amazing NLP trainer who had changed his life. So I decided that as soon as I got back, I was going to find out about this course.

"That's how you produce different results" I said. And I did! The course was brilliant, which is why I'm here now telling you about it.

You see, I realised two things during the training, which changed my life completely.

The first was, if you always do what you've always done, you will always produce the same results. So if you're happy with the results you're producing right now, you don't need to do anything different, it's simple. But if you're not, you have to try something new.

The second thing – well that's the biggie! That's the thing that changed everything forever. Am I glad I went on that course? Of course I am. I believe that if you want to be the best you can be, you have to do something you love, then you're driven to succeed. I can see where I'm going again. That's why I'll keep doing it...

PART ONE

MAXIMISING YOUR PRE-PITCH MEETINGS

1.
WHY YOU NEED TO BRING EMOTIONS INTO YOUR PITCH

IN PART ONE, WE'RE GOING to look at why understanding and communicating emotionally in your pitch, makes you more persuasive and more successful. I'm not saying that you stop using logic to pitch, far from it. I want you to keep using logic. What I'm saying is, that in addition to the way you've been pitching up until now (using your features and benefits) I want you to start thinking about adding emotion to the way you communicate with your clients. Here are a couple of reasons why you need to think about being emotionally persuasive in your pitch.

Firstly, I'm going to assume that at the level you do business, your competitors have similar features and benefits to your own. That your competitors could produce work of a similar standard to yours, and in their pitch they will offer the client similar benefits to the benefits you offer. If these things are true, why is the client going to choose you? You see, selling on your features and benefits alone, doesn't give you the edge, it doesn't make you stand out. In fact, it makes you the same as your competitors.

Secondly, if you annoy or frustrate your client during the pitch, what happens? They disengage from your message. The key is to keep your clients in a positive emotional state. Then they will stay engaged and listening. The other problem associated with this, is that when one client gets offended or annoyed, it's very easy for that emotion to spread amongst their colleagues. Once it spreads, it makes it much harder to re-engage your clients.

Finally, the way we see our future is coloured by the way we feel when we imagine that future. Pitching, by its very nature, is all about your clients' future. You are talking about how you can help them in the future. If they feel annoyed or frustrated, these negative emotions colour the way they see the future you're talking about. But if your clients are in a positive emotional state then they see their future in a positive way, and your pitch is all about how they see their future with you!

2.
HOW TO PREPARE
FOR YOUR PITCH

The power of questions

IF YOU WANT TO BE more successful, if you want to win more pitches, you have to understand your clients emotionally as well as logically. When you do, you will be able to step into their shoes and see and talk about the world the way they see it. This makes you more persuasive.

To be able to do this, assume nothing. Every client is different. I'm always surprised by how many people assume that everyone must be just like them. That people must be interested in what they are interested in. But they're not.

So you have to take time to understand your client's perspective and how they see the world. To do this you have to ask questions and listen to the answers, which allows you to:

- Build trust and empathy.
- Understand your clients' challenges.
- Find a solution to their challenges.
- Know what will motivate them.
- Understand what might put them off you and what might make them like you.

- Understand what they believe can be achieved.
- Make the pitch personal to the key decision makers.
- Be more persuasive.

If you want to ask searching questions and get answers that are of value, you need to create a state of trust between you and your client. You can't just walk up to them and expect them to reveal all, just because you ask them to. You need to nurture them, care about them, be interested in them and build up their trust. When people trust you they will share information with you more freely. The more they trust you, the more they share, and the more they share the more searching your questions can become. By now, I'm hoping that you can start to see the power of good questions and why they are so important.

So, before we get to the questions, we need to look at how we build a deep bond of trust with someone. This bond of trust is called rapport.

What is rapport and why is it important?

People buy people and friends like hanging out with friends.

Clients want to trust the company they hire. They want to get along with them, they want to work with people like them, who care about them, and who have their interests at heart. If you think about it, your friends are like you. They may dress like you and have the same interests as you do, they may even share your beliefs and values. Your friends come to you for advice because they trust you, and because you care about them and have their best interests at heart. Becoming more like your clients, by sharing similar values, beliefs, mannerisms, dress sense, words, interests, ideas, ways of communicating, even spending time together, all helps to build trust.

Rapport allows you to consciously create this bond of trust, and this bond of trust is the start of your emotional connection with your clients. We're going to cover a number of techniques in this chapter, which when you use them, will allow you to shortcut the amount of time it normally takes to build "natural" rapport.

At its most simplistic, rapport is using someone's name or being interested in what they have to say. Of course, it gets a lot more sophisticated than that, and that's what we are going to cover, but first, I wanted to share a story with you, about how even the most basic of rapport building skills can have a powerful impact on someone. This was the first time I used my skills to consciously build a bond of trust with someone.

A number of years ago, a colleague, Adam, who I didn't know that well because I was freelancing at his company, asked me for a drink after work to discuss something. I had never tried a technique known as matching and mirroring, so as you can imagine, I wasn't very good at it. This is what I did, when we went for a drink. If I remembered to, when Adam put his elbow on the table, so did I. Then, when he took his elbow off again, and if I remembered to, I took my elbow off too. And that was the extent of my matching and mirroring. One of the reasons it was so limited was because I was trying to concentrate on what Adam was saying, not what his elbow was doing.

In addition to matching and mirroring Adam, I also repeated back some of his key phrases. I would say something like: "Just so I'm clear about this, are you saying...?" Feeding back what Adam said, conveyed to him that I was listening to him, that I cared about him and that I was genuinely interested in helping him. Which I was.

As you can see, this is a very crude way of building rapport. But, it worked, because as we walked from the bar, Adam turned to me and said: "Marcus, it feels like you're one of the few people who really gets me." When Adam said this, he was expressing more than just his words. He was telling me that he felt comfortable around me, that we had bonded, which apparently, not everyone was able to do. That's the power of rapport, even when it's by someone who had never done it before. This was the start of a good friendship, based on the trust that was established that night.

As I have already said, rapport allows you to create an environment where your clients can trust you.

Where you can ask questions, and elicit answers you might not otherwise be able to. When you get your clients to "open up" to you, you see the world the way they see it. This allows you to tailor your actions and communication so that your client becomes more comfortable when they are around you, which makes further rapport building easier.

The more you can become like your clients, the easier it is for them to trust you.

In the pitch process, you need to start building rapport from your very first interaction with your clients. The longer you have to build rapport, the better the rapport becomes and the more trust you will build.

I'm going to show you how to build rapport in emails, over the telephone, in your pre-pitch meetings and in the pitch itself.

So, let's start by looking at one of the most popular points of contact, emails, and how we build rapport using them.

How to build rapport in emails

Most people are fairly good at rapport in emails. If you're not sure if that's you or not, here are a couple of pointers to consider.

If you are initiating contact with a client you don't know, be friendly. Think about the client, the kind of company they work in, and therefore what information they might be interested in. Present your information in a positive way and get to the point.

If you're responding to an email from a client, you need to match their style. Try to become like them, in your communication with them. If they write short, bullet point emails, you need to do the same. If they write long emails with lots of detail, you need to do the same. Match the way they sign off their email, cheers, thank you, kind regards, best etc. You can match the structure of their emails. For example, respond to the points raised in their email in the same order in which they are raised.

Use the same words or phrases as your client to describe the things or processes they talk about. Many companies have their own "tribal" language. If you adapt your own language to fit it, you're making it easier for them to communicate with you. The more you can match what they do, the better.

Rapport in emails, shows your client how similar you are, how you think like them (structure and bullet points or detail), how you talk like them ("tribal" language and signoff), which makes them more comfortable dealing with you, even if they aren't consciously aware of it.

There is another more advanced way to build rapport in emails which I cover later in Part Two.

How to build rapport over the telephone

Have you ever noticed how some people speak slowly and some people speak quickly? Similarly, have you noticed how some people have a deep voice and some people seem to have a high pitched voice? Speed and tone are two very effective ways of building (or losing) rapport over the phone.

Matching the speed at which someone else speaks during a telephone conversation is the simplest ways of building rapport. If they speak slowly and you speak quickly, slow down to match them, and vice versa. If they speak at an even pace, you need to speak at an even pace. It only needs to be a subtle shift in your speed, for your clients unconscious mind to register that you are like them.

There's another reason why matching someone else's speed during a conversation is important. If you speak quickly to someone who speaks slowly, you will literally overload them with information because they won't be able to process the amount of information they're being given. Likewise, if you speak slowly to someone who speaks quickly, you will really frustrate them, because they will want to finish your sentences.

It's worth noting that no conversation stays at the same speed all the way through. As we get excited, we tend to speed up; as we consider things in more detail, we might slow down. You need to be aware of how the speed of the conversation is changing, and change with it. Although I'm explaining this in a way that means that you will be looking out for those changes of speed, you already do it. It's part of your everyday conversation and I guarantee that you are already brilliant at it. All I'm doing is kicking this idea into your conscious awareness so that you can acknowledge how brilliant you are already and then forget about it again.

Matching tonality is another way to build rapport on the telephone. Most people have a normal tonal range during a conversation. However, if you find yourself speaking to someone with a much deeper or higher tone, it's worth adjusting your tone a little to bring it more into line with the person you're talking to. The idea here is not to suddenly start talking in a strange and unnatural way, but to adjust your own tonal range so it's still comfortable for you.

Building rapport in meetings

Before we get into a process known as matching and mirroring, I need to explain something about it. Many people believe that matching and mirroring is a way to build rapport and to be fair, I did match and mirror my friend Adam, as well as feed back his key phrases, which did build rapport. But, I'm actually going to suggest that matching and mirroring is more a way of telling when you have rapport with someone. The next time you're out with your friends take a moment, step back, and look at what's going on. Everyone will be

22

speaking at the same speed, they will be noisy or quiet, depending on the mood. The chances are that people will be using similar gestures as well as sitting the same way, leaning forward or back, arms crossed or not. Because when we are in rapport with other people, we naturally match their physiology. It happens totally naturally, and it happens all the time. Your friends will have no idea this is happening, and no one is forcing them to be in rapport with each other. The logic is, if it happens naturally, it can be "manufactured" by matching or mirroring someone else's body movements and that's where the idea of matching and mirroring comes from.

If you want to use matching and mirroring to build rapport, you need to reflect back the gestures, movements or body posture of the client with whom you wish to be in rapport.

You can match and mirror their gestures, movements or body posture, in one of two ways. Firstly, you can mirror them. In Mirroring you are presenting a mirror image of your client, back to them. If you stand in front of a mirror, the image that's reflected back is the opposite of you. For example, if I stand in front of the mirror brushing my teeth, my right hand is doing the movement, but in the mirror's reflection, it's my left hand that's doing the movement. When you use mirroring, it's like your client is looking in the mirror and seeing their movements or body posture reflected back to them. If their right hand is up, your left hand is up. If their left leg is crossed, your right leg is crossed.

In matching, all you do is take on the same body posture or movement as your client. If their right hand is up, your right hand is up. If their left leg is crossed, your left leg is crossed. If they scratch the right side of their face, you scratch the right side of your face.

A couple of very important points. This is not mimicking! You are not trying to mimic your client, that's more likely to annoy them than build rapport. The easiest way to avoid mimicking, is to wait for twenty or thirty seconds before you match or mirror what your client has done. This is long enough for your movement to remain outside of their conscious awareness. The other way to avoid mimicking, is to do a smaller version of what they have done (you still need to wait for twenty or thirty seconds). For example, if your client stretches their arms out, even if you wait for a minute and do the same thing, it might still look a little weird! So instead of doing the whole stretch, you could do a much smaller gesture with your arms. Keep it subtle, and leave a pause.

A more advanced way to avoid mimicking is to match something your clients aren't consciously aware of. Most people aren't aware of how often they blink or breathe. This is because it's an unconscious process; it's just something that happens naturally. When you

24

match an unconscious movement, you don't have to wait to do your movement, you can do it straight away. For example, if you want to match someone's breathing rate, the simplest thing to do is breathe out when they are talking, and breathe in when they take a breath. The other way to match breathing rates is to watch your client's shoulders. This is particularly useful in pitches or meetings where your client isn't talking. When their shoulders are going up they are breathing in and when they go down they are breathing out.

The second way to build rapport outside of your client's conscious awareness is to match their blink rate. When they blink, you blink. As with breathing rates, you don't have to wait. No one is aware of when they blink, unless of course, it is pointed out. So, it's a great way to build unconscious rapport.

We've looked at ways of building rapport, but how do you know if you have rapport with your clients? There are two simple ways to check if you have rapport. The first is to Pace and Lead them. Spend a bit of time matching or mirroring your client, build up the rapport. When you think you have it, make an obvious movement, like sitting forward or back, or rubbing your face and see if they do the same or something similar. If they do then it's a fairly good indicator that you have rapport with them – as I said at the start of this section, matching and mirroring is a good rapport indicator, and this is why. The second way to know you have rapport is when you don't notice anything else in the room; it's as if the room falls away and you are just there with the other person and nothing else matters. That's rapport too.

So when you're in your pre-pitch meetings, you need to be building rapport, by really engaging and caring about your client, as well as by matching and mirroring their physiology and tonality in the way we have just talked about.

I wanted to mention one more point about rapport before we get into group rapport. The point is that when you are building rapport using matching and mirroring, you're following what the other person is doing. They are leading your movements. My friend, Rintu Basu, has an interesting and powerful way of reversing this process. When you lead the other person you are taking covert control of the situation. In the same way you might want to check to see if you have rapport, you are taking control. In Rintu's version, you take covert control from the outset. Therefore you are leading your client from the start. There are a number of ways to do this. I'm going to share one with you. Smile. I mean a real, genuine smile, because when you do, something happens. Have you ever been walking down the street and someone smiles at you? What do you do? You smile back. We seem to have a built in tendency to smile back at people when they smile at us. What does this mean? It means that instantly, the person you want to be in rapport with, is actually matching and mirroring you. There's another reason why smiling is so powerful. Our physiology affects our moods. Do we smile because we are happy, or are we happy because we smile? Putting someone into a good mood when you first meet them, will help in more ways than one to start the rapport process. Remember, they might be nervous about meeting you, too. Smiling lets them know that you are happy to meet them, that everything is ok. It's a totally universal, welcoming and a very powerful way of communicating non-verbally. When they respond with a smile, you're becoming like each other –and people buy people they like.

How to build and maintain rapport in groups

One of the most important things when building rapport with groups is to make sure that the first person to present in your pitch is either good at building group rapport, or has a good rapport with the various people in the room. One of the keys to group rapport is to build it as quickly as possible and then maintain it for the entire pitch.

Here are three simple ways to build rapport with groups. Firstly, smile warmly at your clients when you stand up to present. Engage them with your eyes and make them feel welcome. You don't have to start speaking straight away. Take a moment or two to engage your clients. Secondly, you can match what people are doing with their hands. As you stand up to speak, take a look at what the majority of your clients are doing with their hands. As you start speaking, do the same thing. You might notice that people are sitting with their arms crossed, if they are, you could hold your hands together in front of you for a short period of time – this is a smaller version of crossing your arms – and then let your hands fall to the side and see if your clients follow. Thirdly, look out for the rapport leader in a group. This is a person who moves, and creates movement around them. It's like a ripple of movement that the rapport leader starts, that then spreads to others close by. You build rapport with the rapport leader in the same way you build rapport with an individual – using matching and mirroring. When you build rapport with rapport leaders you are automatically building rapport with the people around them. This isn't about seniority, anyone can be a rapport leader within a group. In a training session I gave once, the person who was sitting on my right scratched his face, the person next to him did the same thing. It went all the way around the table to the middle. After the last person scratched their face, I paused briefly and then scratched my cheek as I was talking. I had built rapport with everyone on that side of the room by following what the rapport leader started off. Spotting rapport leaders and building rapport with them, by matching or mirroring what they do, enables you to maintain trust within the group. Which in turn means they are more receptive to the information you are giving them.

So, the first person presenting in your pitch has built rapport with your clients and to maintain that rapport, you need to pass it from presenter to presenter. If the last presenter had good rapport with the client, then the next presenter wants to stand where the previous presenter stood. Go to the same spot in the room and start presenting from there. Unconsciously, this transfers the good rapport from one presenter to another. You can strengthen this rapport transfer, by matching the speed and gestures of the last presenter. If they spoke slowly, you start off speaking slowly, if they did little gestures, you do little gestures. This way the transition between presenters becomes more seamless. However, if the person before you didn't have good rapport and you stand where they stood, you will be taking on their bad rapport. So instead of doing what they did, you want to stand somewhere different to avoid the bad rapport spot. Speak faster if they spoke slowly, use big gestures if they used small ones. In fact, anything to differentiate yourself from the last presenter will let your clients know that you are different. Then you want to start to build rapport with the group all over again.

There is another opportunity to build rapport with your clients that doesn't involve the presenter. Any one of your colleagues can build rapport with an individual or the rapport leader during your pitch, by matching and mirroring them. They can do this as they wait to present or after they have presented. Remember, rapport is built outside conscious awareness, so this is a perfect time to do it.

A note about rapport. To maximise the value of rapport, you need to deliver on the promises you made when you were in rapport. If you promise a fantastic long-term relationship, you need to keep working towards delivering on that promise. Keep building rapport with the client, on the phone, in emails and in meetings. Using rapport to get what you want and then not delivering on your promise harms the relationship more quickly than just about anything else. Of course, not all relationships are perfect all the time, but a good client relationship goes a long way towards smoothing over problems. A bad relationship just makes things worse.

In addition to what we have covered here, you can take rapport in some exciting directions. If you would like to know more, the internet is filled with ideas on rapport. Some of them are useful and some not so useful, so let me direct you to some people I trust to give you great information on rapport (and there's that emotional word again, *trust*). That way if you want to learn more, I know you're in good hands.

I trust three people to give you great advice:

1. Kenrick Cleveland, website: *www.maxpersuasion.com*
2. Kim and Tom, website: *www.essential-skills.com*
3. Rintu Basu, website: *www.thenlpcompany.com*

I have purchased many quality products from all of these people, spent hours reading their material, and ultimately learned a lot of things I wouldn't know about otherwise.

So now you know how to build rapport, it's time to start asking the right questions.

Summary
- You're already a natural at rapport.
- Rapport builds trust, which creates the right environment for your questions and for creating a long-term relationship.
- When you're building rapport, you don't want your client to think you're mimicking them. To avoid this, leave a 20 to 30-second gap.
- You can build rapport in emails, over the telephone (using speed and tone) and in meetings (using matching and mirroring).
- To check you have rapport, try moving and see if your client does a similar movement.
- You can build rapport in groups by smiling and making eye contact when you stand to present. Or by matching what the majority of your clients are doing with their hands. Or by matching or mirroring the rapport leader.

- You pass rapport on, by standing in the same spot as the last presenter and matching their speed or gestures.
- If the last presenter had bad rapport with the group, stand somewhere else and start building rapport again with the group.

Exercises

- The next time you are out with your friends or colleagues, move away from the group and watch how much rapport they have. Are they all speaking at the same speed, sitting or standing in the same way? How are they matching or mirroring each other?
- Practice makes perfect.
- Start by matching your client's email style and language.
- Then try building rapport over the telephone, by matching your client's speed or tone.
- Try matching or mirroring your friends or colleagues. Pick one thing that they do, like I did with Adam, and just do that one thing. Don't try to match and mirror what their arms are doing, as well as the way they sit and the speed at which they speak.
- Start by matching or mirroring and then engage in the conversation. After a couple of minutes, match and mirror them again. Keep going back and building rapport throughout the conversation. Do it in small chunks.
- Once you have mastered matching and mirroring and have built that rapport, notice how you're able to ask more searching questions.

As we're about half way through Part One of this book, I want you to rate how much more persuasive you believe you could be in your next pitch, as a result of the information you now have. Please write your percentage improvement score below.

	%

3.
QUESTIONS THAT
WIN PITCHES

Basic questions

BASIC QUESTIONS ARE ALL THE questions you normally ask in your pre-pitch meeting or Q&A session, with the client. They are the questions that help you to find the best solution to the challenges the client is facing. You're probably already doing this brilliantly, because this is the information you need to build your pitch using features and benefits. Unfortunately, this is also exactly what all your competitors will be doing.

There are two additional basic questions you should ask, if you aren't already:

- Why is the client leaving their current supplier?
- Where does the client want to be in three to five years' time?

The answer to the first question gives you an idea of what not to do or suggest during your pitch – or after it! The next question is about your client's long-term vision and your solution, which ideally needs to move the client towards that vision.

Any solution you outline during your pitch will engage your clients emotionally. But they will only be emotionally engaged at a company level. There is another way to engage with your clients at a much deeper emotional level and my advanced questions will help you to do this, because they make your pitch personal to your individual clients.

The advanced questions that make it personal

If the basic questions give you the "must have" information, advanced questions allow you to understand your individual clients at an emotional level. As you will see, this allows you to influence their logical decisions. Before we look at the questions, I need to explain, by looking at a communications model, why they make you more influential.

The Hierarchy of Influence, looks at how our logical decisions are influenced by our emotions. It is based upon Rintu Basu's development of Robert Dilts' Neurological Levels.

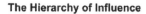

The Hierarchy of Influence

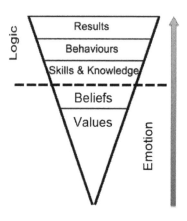

Starting at the top of the Hierarchy of Influence are results. We all produce results; sometimes we produce results we want and sometimes we don't, but we're still producing results. For us to produce these results, we have to do something, we have to take action: these are our Behaviours. Therefore, our behaviours influence the results we produce. Below Behaviours we have Skills and Knowledge. Our skills and knowledge have a direct influence on our behaviours, which in turn influence the results we produce. Everything at this level is based on logic. There are Key Performance Indicators (KPIs) and processes for measuring and evaluating results and performances.

When you pitch using features and benefits, you are selling at this logical level. Your features are your skills and knowledge. They are the type of product or service you offer, your IP, the number of offices you have, the quality and experience of your employees, in fact anything that defines your Unique Selling Proposition. Depending on your product or service you will either be influencing the behaviour of a third party, usually the general public or your client's employees, to produce positive results.

The benefits to your client are the results you are able to produce for them. You're influencing behaviour to produce these positive results for your clients.

You have to use logical arguments in your pitch, so your clients understand your solution and how it benefits them.

Below the dotted line we have our beliefs. What we believe about ourselves and what we can achieve in our lives have a direct bearing on what kind of skills and knowledge we might acquire. If I believe that I'm hopeless at maths I'm not going to bother sitting exams to become an accountant, which, in turn, affects the results that I will produce in my life.

Below beliefs, we have our values. Our values are the things that motivate our behaviour. They're what is important to us. If we're not motivated to do something it's because it's not that important to us, so we put it off, sometimes altogether. Our values also have a direct influence on the results we produce.

Our beliefs and values are based on emotion. The closer you're able to communicate with an individual's beliefs and values, the more influence you have over their logical decisions. You need to use emotions in your pitch, because they commit your client to your solution. In the following sections, we're going to look at how you can elicit your client's beliefs and values, and use them to create a commitment to you, your company and your solution.

I have developed three simple questions, which literally unlock your client's hidden beliefs and values. They are the Three Golden Questions.

Three Golden Questions

Here are the Three Golden Questions you can ask:
1. What is important to you about...?
2. Is there any reason why you might not hire us?
3. Why are we on your pitch list?

On the face of it they really don't sound that impressive. And that's what makes them so powerful. If they don't sound like much, then they are easier for your clients to answer without being aware of the information they are giving away.

Understanding and eliciting Values – the First Golden Question

Our values are what motivate us to do the things we do. You will be reading this book, because it's important to you to win more business or to understand how you can use emotion to be more successful in your pitch.

Because our values are our primary source of motivation, we can't go against them. They are so deeply rooted within our personality, that when you elicit a value statement and attach it to your product or service, the individual client will be powerfully motivated to buy from you.

There are two ways of eliciting a values statement from your clients. You can do it overtly, or covertly. I'm going to start with the overt way, because it's the most straightforward. It's the first of my Three Golden Questions.

To elicit a value you ask: "What's important to you about...?" All you do is name the thing you want to elicit a value about. Here are some examples:

- What's important to you about the agency/supplier you're going to be working with?
- What's important to you about the work that you do?
- What's important to you about the work you're looking for?
- What's important to you about the ideas we're putting forward?

You could put anything after "What's important to you about...?" Whatever reply you get will be their value statement about your question.

Let's say you ask:

"What's important to you about the company you're going to hire?" and they answer: "I want a company which will increase my sales. "Increasing sales is the most important, personal motivator for that individual client.

You want to get values statements from as many key decision makers as you can. If you can only get value statements from half, get them for the most influential half. Obviously, if you can get more go for it. The more you have, the more effectively you can communicate during your pitch.

Key points when eliciting values statements:

1. Build rapport before asking questions, especially where you're eliciting a value. We've already looked at how and why rapport allows you to build a bond of trust. You need to make the value elicitation seem natural; you don't want to draw attention to the importance of this question.

2. You might need to soften the way you ask the question. Just coming out with "What's important to you...?" again and again might seem a little odd. Here's how you soften the question. "So we can help you better, what's important to you about...?" or, "So we can understand you better as a client, what's important to you about...?"

3. You really need to ask this question as part of a larger conversation where you're asking a lot of other questions. This way it gets hidden and will appear innocuous.

4. One way to do this is to ask different value elicitation questions of the key decision makers. You might want to ask procurement: "What's important to you about keeping costs down?" You might want to ask the CEO: "What's important to you about the agency you are looking to hire?" You might want to ask the Marketing Director: "What's important to

you about more sales?" Keeping the questions different will help to disguise what you are doing.

5. As soon as you get an answer to the values question, write it down and memorise it. Why? Because you want to use their exact words, not your interpretation, not what you think they said, but what they actually said. In exactly the right order and sequence your client used. The words we use mean something unique to us. If you interpret your client's value statement, it's not their statement any more. It has no power or relevance to them at all, it's just more talk in your pitch. That's why, when you attach a value statement to the pitch you have to use their exact words.

6. It doesn't matter if there are a couple of weeks or even months between eliciting a value statement and attaching it. In fact, sometimes it's better to have a gap between the elicitation and attaching the value, because it makes what you're doing a little less obvious.

7. You will notice that the values elicitation question contains the words "to you". This makes it personal to the client and they will give you a personal answer. If you want to elicit a company value, you simply ask: "What's important to your company about...?"

That's how you elicit a value statement in an overt way. It's actually very simple to do because you're only asking, "What's important to you about...?"

Now, let's look at how you might elicit a values statement in a covert way. Here's what you do. In any conversation people will be giving you information about themselves. As you listen, pick out things that might be important to them. Once you start listening for those values statements, you will be amazed at what you hear.

In your pre-pitch meetings, you should do the same thing. To help you listen out for information that might be important to the client, look out for phrases like these: "I/we want to..." or "I/we have to..." or "I/we need to...".

When you hear something you think is important to the client, all you do is ask: "Is that something that's important to you?" or "Is that the most important thing to you?" In a meeting the other day, a client said, "I don't have a lot of time, so we need to get going quickly." I responded by asking if time was important to her. She said it was. I changed my sales pitch and put the effective use of time as a key benefit of working with me. When I did this, I was attaching her value of having limited time to my offer. More about attaching values shortly.

You can even pre-empt a covert values elicitation by asking questions like: "What do you want to get from our relationship?" followed by, "Is that one of the most important things to you?" If they say yes, you have elicited their value. If they say no, just leave it. They will probably say something later on in the conversation that might give you their value.

My preferred method is to listen out for values statements during a meeting and if, by the end of the meeting, I haven't heard any, I just ask the overt question: "So we can understand you better, what's important to you about...?"

Another simple way to elicit a value statement – and it's great if you're not sure exactly what to elicit – is just to ask: "So what's important to you?" and let the client fill in the blanks for you. Whatever they say will be their values statement within the context of your conversation at that moment.

Attaching Values in your pitch

So, you've got this golden nugget, the thing that can move a mountain or at least powerfully motivate your client. How do you use it to affect your client's behaviour in your favour?

The most powerful way to use a value statement in your pitch is to link it to a part of your presentation, but not just any part. As you work through the presentation, there will be places where your content is more specific to one individual client than anyone else. This is where you link their value statement and, if possible, link it specifically to a slide that has the greatest benefit for that individual.

Let's say you have a fabulous, benefit driven slide in your presentation for the Marketing Director. You've already elicited the Marketing Director's value statement in your pre-pitch meetings, which was to have sustainable results. You're talking about these results in the Marketing Director's section and you come to the benefit slide, the one he's been waiting for. This is how you attach his value statement to your product or service, and personally I'm in favour of the direct approach. So, make sure you have good eye contact with him and say something like this: "In the pre-pitch meetings, you told us that you wanted sustainable results from our solution and we believe, with the figures you're looking at here, we can deliver you exactly that."

Bingo!

You have just linked his value statement to the results he wanted, your results. He's hooked.

Sometimes, if you have elicited a very personal values statement from a client, it might be a good idea to attach it covertly. The idea is to attach a values statement without making your clients feel embarrassed. To do this, you still want to link the value to the benefits slide in your presentation, just in a more subtle way. You could try something like this: "We wanted to show you a way of generating

QUESTIONS THAT WIN PITCHES

sustainable results and, as you can see here, we believe these results will allow you to..." The result will be the same because you're still attaching their value to your product or service.

There are a couple of other covert ways of attaching values. You can attach a value statement in vox pops (a video interview with a member of the public). This way you are using actual customers to attach your client's value to your product or service. If the Marketing Director thinks consumer vox pops offer important insights, this might be a very powerful way to attach his or her value statement to one of your ideas. If, during the clip, the person talks about how great it would be if the product did ABC (something you're suggesting), because they think that it would make the product more sustainable, the customer has attached the Marketing Director's value statement for you. In addition, if you are offering a number of ideas in your pitch and want your client to choose one idea over the others, attaching values statements only to the idea you want to be selected, will make it the most likely option to be picked.

Another idea, along similar lines, is for you to use a testimonial in your pitch to support a key point. In this testimonial you get the person talking about how your ideas made their results more sustainable. You've just done it again. I'm sure you can come up with lots of other examples of how you could attach a values statement in your pitch.

If you are concerned about eliciting and attaching a values statement, don't be. It's easy. I'm sure you could ask someone: "what's important to you about...?" Like everything, the key is to try it out with friends or colleagues and see how it works for you. Practise, have fun with it.

Linking a value statement to a benefit or result is the most effective way to use this technique, but it's not the only way. Let me give you another example of something that happened to me. I was interested in going on a course. To do this, the company requested that I complete an online form. This consisted of three questions: Name, Email address and What's important to you about coming on this course? To which I replied, "Helping people". Of course, at that point I didn't realise that they were eliciting a value statement from me. Shortly afterwards, I got an email from them saying: "Thank you for considering us and so that you know that you're making the best decision, would you like to come and meet us, to see if you like the trainers, the course and the type of students we have?" Of course I emailed back to say, yes. A date was set and at the appointed hour, I arrived to see if I liked the course. I remember having a great chat with a trainer and a few other people, and then seeing what they were doing. It all looked great. They asked me if I wanted to enrol. Normally it would take me at least a week before I could commit to anything like that – and because it was an expensive course you could probably add in a few more days just so I could be sure. But, in a very uncharacteristic moment, I got out my chequebook and handed over a deposit there and then. How had they done it? All they had done was attached my value statement from the online questionnaire to their course. Most of the conversation was just general chat (rapport building), but somewhere in that chat they said, "This course is great if you're interested in helping people." Bingo. They had attached my value to their course. Of course they made sure that course was right for me first; that it was something I would genuinely benefit from; that I would enjoy doing it and that I could afford it. Getting to know me, understanding what was important to me and making sure I believed I was doing the right thing for the right reason was all part of this conversation. They asked lots of questions and I gave lots of answers. I liked them, they cared about me and, like most people, I like to be cared about. And I guess they must have liked me too because they wanted to have me on their course. I really loved it! In fact, that course changed my life. Here's a final interesting point about this story. If they didn't want me to join, they would simply have attached a different value to their course. I would have walked away none the wiser, just thinking to myself that it wasn't the course for me.

A final point before we leave Values. What do you do if you really can't get any values statements from your clients? I'm going to assume you've tried, but have been genuinely unable to elicit anything. Here are a couple of ideas.

Find a client you're currently working with, preferably from the same industry or someone with similar needs to your client, and ask them. If you can't do this, try the internet. Most companies have information about themselves, their values or beliefs, somewhere on their site. A good place to look is in the "about us" section or their company blog, if they have one. Similarly, companies often have a presence on video sites or other social media platforms. All of these sites will give you useful information. How about looking in the trade press? Companies like to have articles published about them. Or how about talks they might have done for their trade body or local business groups? Finally, how about talking to someone who used to work for your client? A previous Board member who has moved on might be willing to meet for lunch to help you, or have a telephone conversation with you. Or, how about your client's PR agency; you could be honest and say what you're doing, or you could be just a little more covert, to glean information. My point is that in this day and age there are lots of ways of getting information about people and companies. Building up a picture of your client is an essential part of the process, and in all of this information will be their values. The chances are you might get a hit and, if you do, you're better off than you were before. If you don't, then you've lost nothing.

So, by meeting their values, you've given the key decision makers personal reasons for hiring you and in your solution you've given them plenty of company reasons for hiring you too.

Understanding beliefs

In this section, I'm going to simplify beliefs and tailor the information I'm giving you, to fit the purposes of this book.

A belief is a statement or thought that is believed to be true for the person expressing it. The key ingredient in any belief is emotion.

We all hold beliefs about everything, from our own abilities, to the way the world works around us. A belief is neither good, nor bad, neither right nor wrong. However, a belief either supports us, or it doesn't.

At one end of the scale, I believe that the world revolves around the sun, that birds fly South in winter and that the sun rises in the East and sets in the West. These are all beliefs I have about the world I live in. I don't have much emotion attached to them, but I do believe them to be true. At the other end, are beliefs that I am emotionally attached to. If I believe that I am a terrible presenter, the result might be that I try to avoid presenting at all costs, for fear of looking stupid or foolish. At an extreme, I might not take a job because it involved me having to present and having to present makes me nervous, feel sick with worry and lacking in confidence (lots of emotion).

If, however, I believe I'm a great presenter, I might seek out opportunities to present because I really enjoy it. I love standing in front of people and giving them information that empowers them. It makes me feel alive. At an extreme, I might get extra coaching on presenting so I could be even better at it.

These are two different beliefs, causing two different types of behaviour. Here's why beliefs are important to you in terms of winning business. Everyone behaves in accordance with the beliefs they hold. If I believe I'm terrible at presenting, I'm not suddenly going to start presenting. This happens because, the more emotionally attached I am to my belief, the more that belief drives my behaviour.

In a pitch, your clients will hold two beliefs about you and your company. They are either beliefs that support you, or they are beliefs that don't support you. The beliefs that don't support you are known as limiting beliefs, because they limit what your client thinks you can do and because they limit the actions your client will be prepared to take to support you.

Your client's beliefs are shaped by things they have read about you, things they have been told about you, meetings they have had with you and their past experiences of dealing with companies like yours. When your client is looking for a supplier to work with they are putting their brand's future, and potentially their own success, in someone else's hands. By the very nature of the situation, it's going to be an emotional decision for them, so you can guarantee that your client will be behaving in a way that supports the beliefs they hold about you. That's why identifying and understanding your client's beliefs is crucial to your pitch process.

Beliefs and pitching – the Second and Third Golden Questions

In your pitch, you need to neutralise the limiting beliefs your client holds about you. And you need to capitalise on their beliefs that support you.

Let's start by looking at limiting beliefs. There are two ways of determining what limiting beliefs your clients might hold about you. Firstly, you can ask the second Golden Question:

"Are there any reasons why you wouldn't hire us?"

Or: "Are we weak in any areas?"

Or: "Could we do better in any areas?"

When you ask one of these, or similar questions, the answer you get from your client is a limiting belief expressed in terms of a concern or objection. If they haven't worked with you before, then it's only their perception of you. If they have worked with you before then their limiting belief is based upon their actual experience. This means that they are more emotionally attached to this belief and you will therefore need to apply a combination of the ideas outlined below in order to neutralise it.

I have two important points to make about asking the second Golden Question. Firstly, as I've said before, you have to establish a good level of rapport before asking questions like these. Secondly, choose your moment. If you have an opportunity to test your ideas with the client before the pitch, this is a good time to ask the second Golden Question, because in that meeting, your client's mindset is one of offering help and advice.

The second way to determine a limiting belief is to review your previous pitches and look for recurring challenges or objections raised by the client. These are your client's limiting beliefs about what you can achieve.

Your client might not voice these limiting beliefs out loud, but that doesn't mean they're not thinking about them. Your pitch objective is to neutralise the biggest limiting beliefs your client holds about you. If you don't neutralise these limiting beliefs, you are leaving in place the barriers that stop them from buying your product or service. By removing their limiting beliefs, your client has to behave in a manner that supports any other beliefs they hold about you. If you neutralise the limiting beliefs, your client is only left with supporting beliefs. The more supportive beliefs they hold about you, the more your client has to support you with their logical decisions and behaviours.

Before I tell you how to do this during the pitch process, I need to explain one more thing. The way you neutralise a limiting belief is by breaking it up sufficiently for a new, better belief to take its place. This is the key. If your client doesn't think that the new belief you are offering them is better than that which they currently hold, they will reject it. Similarly, pushing back on a limiting belief, often only serves to antagonise or entrench your clients position further. Arguments are a good example of two opposing beliefs, where each side's position becomes increasingly more entrenched. Neutralising a limiting belief takes more than just logical understanding. That's why you will have greater success if you use indirect, covert ways to neutralise them.

So how do you do this? There are a number of ways you can start to break up a limiting belief. Here are a few ideas:

1. **Resolve the clients concerns in a conventional way.** If your clients think you are too expensive, can you reduce your price? If they don't like your solution, how could you change it to bring it more into line with what they are looking for? You need to do the obvious things first. Then, during the pitch process, reinforce it by adding in something from the list below.

2. **Actions speak louder than words.** In this day and age, it's common for clients to feel let down by their suppliers. The road is littered with broken promises. If this is how your client feels, before the pitch, offer to do a couple of things over and above what they might reasonably expect or ask for. This way you demonstrate to them, that, if you promise them something, you will deliver on that promise. This is just one way you could use this concept, I'm sure you can think of others. It's worth noting that you don't want to use this idea in isolation, because on its own it's not enough to neutralise a limiting belief.

3. **Testimonials** are a great way of using social proof to demonstrate that you can do the things you say you can do. I have a preference for video testimonials because they make the limiting belief and therefore your solution, real for the client. Testimonials go a long way towards neutralising a limiting belief. To use them effectively, find a client you're currently working with (who shared the

same concerns as your client), who's gone through your process and realised that their concerns were unfounded. This leaves a very powerful impression on your client. Especially if everything ran the way you said it would, or better! We cover testimonials in more detail in Part Three.

4. **Details.** Giving a detailed outline of the steps you would take, helps your clients feel more confident about the things that are troubling them. Because giving details implies that you have done this before and allows you to point out how you would avoid the pitfalls. This helps to take away any doubt about your ability. Another advantage of giving details is that clients become nervous about things they don't understand or can't see clearly. Giving your clients details, allows them to picture their part in the process. The issue then moves from what they are worried about, to whether or not they like the process you've outlined. If they are thinking about that, their original concern is no longer relevant.

5. **Metaphors.** It's easy to tell a metaphor (story) based upon your client's limiting belief. This enables you to talk about the limiting belief in a totally covert way, without actually directly mentioning the issue. To your client it's just a story, so you can tell it anywhere in the pitch process without arousing suspicion. We go into

metaphors in much more detail in Part Three, so I'm only going to give you a brief example here. If your client has a limiting belief about moving their (global) business to your company, you could tell a story like this:

"I don't know if you remember, but around Easter 2010, Europe was literally shutdown by volcanic ash from Iceland. I was on holiday with my family in Southern Spain, and like many families, we got stranded abroad. It was a terrible time because no one knew what was going on. There were lots of families who didn't know what to do. When you have small children or babies, which a lot of people did, you really need to be able to make plans so they don't suffer. I remember after the second day the planes were grounded, people started to get really worried, families were just stranded in the airport, no one was looking after them. I needed to get back to work on an important project and the children had school starting in a couple of days. I called Sally, my PA, to see if she could do anything, only to discover that five or six other colleagues were also stuck abroad and couldn't get back. Sally said she would call back as soon as she had some news. So we waited like everyone else, not sure what was going to happen. It's not easy when you don't know how you're going to get back. We prepared ourselves for the worst.

Long waits, disappointment, chaos. That was a long day. When Sally called back, she had somehow managed to get us on a train back to Calais. It would take a day and a half but we were so relieved, it felt so good to know everything was going to be ok. I don't know how she did it, but she managed to get everyone back one way or another as quickly as she could."

In this metaphor (which I don't recommend you use because you're not the only person to read this book), your client, is me and my family. They probably see themselves as a "global family" anyway. The airlines are your competition. Sally is obviously your company. The family is stranded abroad, which represents your client's brand. They want to move everyone to one company, to bring them "home". The story is based on a real event, which gives it more credibility. And it was real for a huge amount of people, so there's no reason to suspect that it couldn't have happened to me. The point of a metaphor is to tell the story and then leave it, don't explain it. Our minds are always looking for meaning, so your metaphor is designed to sit in your clients mind, percolating away, until they make a conscious or unconscious link between their limiting belief and the hidden message contained within your metaphor.

6. **Pacing and Leading.** This technique allows you to gain agreement by first showing the client that you understand their position, and then moving it. You can pace your client's limiting beliefs and then lead them, by making a suggestion they can buy into. If your client is worried about being let down, here's an example of how you could pace and lead that concern: "There are lots of companies out there who make claims they can't meet. We know, because we, like you, have had the misfortune of working with a number of them. And we've found that there's nothing more frustrating. That's why we won't work with companies who do that, we believe it's unacceptable because we don't do it". In this example, I have paced the client's frustration about being let down, and led them by suggesting that it's something we don't tolerate either, that's why it would never happen with us. Again, we cover Pacing and Leading in Part Two.

7. **Use a conversational pre-frame.** A pre-frame is a way of addressing your clients limiting belief before you get to it in your pitch. There are many ways of looking at a limiting belief and the job of a pre-frame is to offer a better way of looking at it. When you use a pre-frame, it has to be realistic for your client otherwise they will just reject it. I used a pre-frame at the beginning of this section on *understanding beliefs*. There are lots of examples of

pre-frames in our everyday lives. Here's a common one from retail: *"Buy now, pay in twelve months"*. This pre-frame is designed to overcome the concern about the item being unaffordable now. It literally says, don't worry about paying us now, you can pay in the future when you can afford it. It's a great introduction into the first type of pre-frame. A "future focused" pre-frame allows you to neutralise a limiting belief by talking about an event, out in the future, past the problem, where the limiting belief is no longer relevant. This type of pre-frame is extremely useful in your pitch. As an example, many clients have concerns about moving their account and all the upheaval it might cause. In your introduction you could focus their attention on the end result rather than their concerns. "We live in a world where change seems to be happening more rapidly than that at which we can sometimes reasonably keep up and whilst we are in the throes of change it can be easy to lose sight of the long-term objectives. So, let's focus on where we need to get to, not on what might stop us from getting there. And what we need to focus on are your brand objectives." Or, "The world is changing around us. We can stand still and hope it doesn't affect us or we can change with it. Either way we need to keep your future in mind – that future where your brand objectives are the necessity that drives the change you want." In both cases, I have used the change that the client knows must occur as a way of focusing them onto the future results they want. The second example of a pre-frame, links two concepts together. Here is another example I've used to encourage people to look at presenting in a different way. "If you're standing up here, then you are getting paid. If you're sitting down, then you are paying. Think about it. The theatre, cinema, concerts, presenting information. Pretty much in any situation, if you are standing up and delivering information, you are being paid. But if you're sitting down, you're paying. Now, who wants to go through life being paid and who wants to go through life paying?" In this example, I have linked the thing that I want them to do, standing up, to something positive – making money – and then linked the thing I don't want them to do, stay sitting down, to something negative (paying). Now, most people in life want to make money, so I have given them a positive association around standing up and presenting, and because it's true, it's easy for them to believe.

Finally, I have to share an example of a great pre-frame that happened totally by accident during a meeting I had with a client. I had gone to talk to my client about a proposal I had, to help people find an opportunity to work in the countryside.

The meeting was going really well, I had great rapport with everyone and we were in agreement about the need for this service. Then the MD said that she couldn't see how the idea could be monetised. We talked about our options with regard to this, then they asked me what I wanted to get paid for my time. Whatever I had in my head before the meeting had been completely pre-framed by the monetising comment. I stumbled a bit and talked around the subject before saying that they could decide. It was a brilliant example of an unintentional pre-frame.

The question now is, how do you prevent this happening to you? The answer is simple, have a strong example of how your client can get a great return on investment (ROI) from your ideas; spell it out for them. If you're a client and you want to reduce your suppliers' fees, just point out to them that you can't see how their idea can be monetised or produce the ROI you want. They have nowhere to go when it comes to talking about their fee. I recently tried the reverse of this pre-frame in a meeting with a new client. I wanted to pre-frame my fees, because when an individual is paying they can seem expensive. When we met, I started by asking him about what he wanted and how I could help. I built rapport and when I knew that he was interested in my product, I used a powerful linking pre-frame. I knew I had the right product for this client, so I demonstrated a little bit more of my offer, to get him excited about what he could learn. Then, when he could see how much money he could make from my help, I pointed out that this product would only really benefit someone who was experienced in sales (which he was) and someone who was already successful. By this point in the process, he wanted to know more about my product and so he agreed to being experienced and successful. By getting him to admit he was successful, I had pre-framed the conversation I was going to have about my fees. A couple of things to note: I didn't only use the pre-frame to neutralise any limiting beliefs about my fees; and more importantly, I knew I could really help this client, which I have subsequently done. He's very happy with the results I helped him to achieve.

8. **Be calm and authoritative.** When you get to your client's limiting belief in the pitch, if you are calm and authoritative you're playing down their fears. People who are calm and have authority, tend to speak slowly and use slower, more considered gestures. People who are nervous tend to speak quickly and fidget. By slowing down and having an air of authority you convey confidence. If you are confident about the challenge, your clients are more likely to be, too.

9. **Use a linguistic re-frame.** A re-frame is reactive, because it challenges the limiting belief after you have heard it. It works in the same way as a pre-frame, in as much as it offers another way of looking at the limiting belief. Most of our everyday sayings are re-frames. One in the hand is worth two in the bush. Buy cheap, buy twice. Don't look a gift horse in the mouth. Every cloud has a silver lining. We're literally bombarded by re-frames every day. By our friends and family, work colleagues, even television. You're already using re-frames and you're probably using them in your pitches, as well. Advertising has harnessed the power of the re-frame (and pre-frame) in a masterful way. An advertising campaign is a series of re-frames, set around the same theme, with slightly different messages. Each different message is designed to re-frame your opinion of the product. Eventually you have been offered enough re-frames to change your belief about the product and give it a try. You can apply the same ideas to your pitch. What limiting beliefs do you need to re-frame for your client? Then all you do is present your ideas in a way that allows you to re-frame your client's objections during the pitch. Remember all you are doing is offering them another, better way to look at the concern.

The other kind of re-frame that many people will be familiar with, are political re-frames. They are known more appropriately as "spin". Personally, I think that political re-frames/spin tend to annoy people, rather than re-frame concerns or challenges they may have. This is mainly because they are shallow and transparent as spin, and more importantly, because they miss one critical ingredient, emotion. Politicians tend to throw out re-frames based on logic, because they are usually defending a budget cut, or political decision. The re-frames used in advertising are more powerful because they re-frame the emotion that is contained within the belief. Advertisers spend millions on focus groups, to get to the very core of an issue; that's why their reframes are so effective. If you really want your re-frames to have a powerful effect on your clients, you have to understand the emotion contained within the limiting belief. You don't need to spend millions on research to develop your own powerful re-frames, just try your ideas out on your colleagues before you present them to your clients. The reason why our common sayings work as re-frames is because they are said in the right emotional context. When the listener hears the re-frame, they are emotionally moved by it. That's why they change their behaviour.

As I said earlier, you want to neutralise your client's biggest limiting beliefs. If you can neutralise a couple, great; if you only neutralise one, that's better than nothing. I'm going to recommend that you don't use the same technique all the time. Get creative. Use ideas in combination to strengthen their effect. The more strongly held the belief is, the more techniques you need to combine to neutralise it. I'm going to recommend that you try at least three of these techniques in conjunction with each other for neutralising a limiting belief. You need to start the process in the pre-pitch meetings if you can and then build from there. You don't want to leave neutralising a limiting belief until it arises in your pitch. Be proactive, use a pre-frame, metaphor or actions, to start the process, but bear in mind that the idea is to be covert when neutralising beliefs. If your client gets wind of what you are doing, the barriers come down and they will disengage.

Before you read on, stop for a minute and think about this book in terms of beliefs. Because if you think about it, this whole book is about re-framing what you believe you can achieve, and installing a new set of supportive beliefs in you. All I'm doing is using the techniques I'm outlining to help you believe that you will be better at winning pitches.

As well as neutralising limiting beliefs, you also want to capitalise on any supportive beliefs your client holds about you – and they must hold some about you otherwise why are you on the pitch list?

To find out what supporting beliefs your client holds about you, you need to ask the third and final Golden Question:

"Why are we on your pitch list?" Or in a slightly softer way: "Thank you for putting us on the pitch list. We were just interested to know why you asked us to tender."

Whatever your clients say will be their supporting belief about you and the thing you need to capitalise on. It's a good idea, if you can, to start to capitalise on this supporting belief as soon as possible. You don't have to go over the top, but you do want to give examples of your services or products that reinforce why they are interested in you. A good covert way to do this in your pitch is in a testimonial. Get the person in the testimonial to talk about how you helped them achieve more of the supporting belief your client holds about you. For example, if the client is coming to you because you can help them win awards, the person in the testimonial should talk about how you helped them win awards.

Sometimes, there's an official body between you and the client, who selects the companies for the pitch. If you can't get to the client, ask this official body. They must have selected you for some reason and you need to find out that reason.

At the very least, armed with the information that you now have, I hope that you won't make the mistake of trampling all over your clients' beliefs and values and thereby destroying your chances of winning. Beliefs and values are one of the few things that we will all stand up for at any cost. They are at the core of our very being. To put it another way, everything that you experience in this world, the way that you see the world and even how successful you become, is down to the beliefs you hold about yourself and the world you live in, which is why understanding beliefs is so important.

If you can't neutralise a limiting belief, don't fight against it. If your client can't get beyond their belief, honour it. Agree with them, at least this way you won't be alienating them. If you're the incumbent in a pitch, the beliefs held by your client will be well founded to them, even if they aren't to you. They have worked with you. They know what you're like and whether you keep the promises you make. If you try to convince them that they are wrong, this will only antagonise them. So why not surprise them, and agree with them? It's easier to agree with your clients and then try to move their position, than to say that they're wrong and blunder on. If you agree to not always having done the best you could, then you have somewhere to go.

I had an interesting conversation a while back about this. A company I was helping to pitch, wanted to know my thoughts on dealing with a client who really liked their current supplier. My advice was to agree with the client. At the start of the pitch, point out how good their current supplier is and how they have helped them. I even suggested they list the ways that made their supplier so good. This relaxes the client, because they're agreeing with what is being said (this is a pacing statement). They weren't coming in saying: "We're better than what you have right now, because..." which will only annoy the client. During the pitch, they started to slowly give examples where they could do a better job, which started to unpick everything that the current supplier was good at doing in a covert way (leading them). Being subtle when you unpick what their supplier does, means you're not frustrating or annoying the client.

The importance of self-belief in your pitch

The final type of belief in a pitch is your own self-belief. This belief is just as important as the other types of beliefs, if not more so. You have to believe absolutely in your product and how it can help your client reach their personal or brand objectives. You also have to believe that you can win. Most people are familiar with the idea that if you don't believe in what you're selling, neither will your client. Here's why.

You unconsciously communicate your thoughts through your non-verbal communication (how you use your gestures, your body language, facial expressions and tonality) and because this is done unconsciously, you have no control over what or how it manifests itself. If you don't believe in what you are selling, your body language and tonality will reflect this. Your words won't be congruent with your non-verbal communication and we all spot these non-verbal cues and react to them, rather than the words we use.

Most people say that you have to believe in your product, and they think that's enough. Well, it's a good start, but I'm going to recommend that you take it a stage further. Believing in your product will give you one level of non-verbal communication. The next level, is to believe that your product or service is invaluable to the welfare of your client. This leads to a change in your mindset, and that change sets-up a chain reaction in the choice of words you use, the way you stand or sit, your gestures, the way you say what you say, and even the way you introduce yourself.

You want to believe that your product or service can help your clients to live longer, be happier, be richer, be more successful, get promoted, find more clients, etc. You have to be convinced that you have something that will help your clients achieve the things they most want in their lives. When you are convinced, all of your non-verbal communication will reflect this, and this will help to convince your clients too.

So what do you do if you really don't believe in what you're pitching? If you can't see how your product or service could help to benefit your client? If this were me,

I wouldn't get involved in the pitch, but that's me. Clients pick up things like this. But, if you really are irreplaceable, then there is something you could try. Start by asking yourself, what's really stopping me from believing our product or service can benefit this client? Why can others believe in it, when I can't? Take a couple of people to one side and ask them why they believe in what they're pitching (you don't have to tell them why you're doing this). This will at least give you a starting point to work from. If you're still having trouble, and as a last resort, I suggest you only present information that you totally believe in. That way at least your non–verbal communication will be congruent with what you're saying.

Believing your product can have a positive impact on your client's welfare or wellbeing is all part of your ability to believe you can win – and believing you can win is critical as well. Clients want to work with winners, people who believe in themselves and their offer.

Imagine for a moment that you're the client, sitting in a pitch. Everything you're seeing and hearing is valuable and helpful to you and your company. But as you sit there, the presenters, one after another, just don't seem... well it's probably hard to put your finger on. It's like they just don't believe in themselves, they don't seem to believe they can win. Now, would you want to work with a company like that?

You have to have self-belief, in your product or service and in your ability to win.

Summary

- Logic creates understanding. Emotion creates commitment to your product or service.

- Your competitors are asking the basic questions.

- The Three Golden Questions (advanced questions) make your pitch personal and more emotional for your clients.

- You have to have rapport with your clients before you ask the Three Golden Questions.

- You can elicit and attach values in your pitch, either overtly or covertly.

- You have to use your client's exact words when you're attaching their value statement to your product or service, in your pitch.

- Everyone has different values; if you can, elicit different values for the key decision makers.

- There are two types of beliefs held by the clients.

- Limiting beliefs are the barriers to winning the pitch.

- You can neutralise limiting beliefs by using a combination of, actions, testimonials, details, metaphors, Pacing and Leading, pre-frames, being calm and authoritative and re-frames.

- Supporting beliefs are why the client has chosen you; you need to capitalise on them during your pitch process.

- The final type of belief in your pitch is the belief you hold about yourself and your product. You have to believe you can win and that your product will make a real difference to the wellbeing of your client. When you do, your non-verbal communication reflects this belief.

Exercises

- People are expressing their values and beliefs all the time. Get good at listening out for them.
- Practise the eliciting of values statements from friends and colleagues, either covertly or overtly.
- Then attach their values to something you have (a book or product) or something you're doing (going on a trip, going out), and see what happens.
- Start to capitalise on supporting beliefs people hold about you. If a colleague thinks you're good at something, prove it to them.
- Similarly, if people think you are bad at something, try to pre-frame or re-frame their belief.

As we leave Part One of this book, I want you to rate how much more persuasive you believe you could be in your next pitch, as a result of the information you now have. Please write your percentage improvement score below.

	%

.

PART TWO

DESIGNING
EMOTIONALLY
PERSUASIVE
CONTENT

1.
CREATING IMPACT

RAPPORT CREATES THE ENVIRONMENT IN which your clients trust you enough to be taken on an emotional journey with you. Your pitch is the emotional journey.

Designing your emotional content

One of the most important elements in effective communication is the way you structure your content. Of course, it has to be logical enough so your clients understand your solution, but it also has to take into account what emotions you want your clients to feel as you take them through your pitch. As I keep saying, you need to keep your clients in a positive emotional state. This doesn't mean that you want them cheering and clapping all the way through your pitch, that's not going to be that helpful because it's unsustainable. More importantly, there are better emotional states for people to be in when they learn new information.

As you design your pitch content, it will help you to be aware of the emotional states you're putting your clients through. There are a number of useful emotions to consider:

- Curiosity
- Interest
- Pride
- Anticipation
- Excitement
- Relief
- Commitment
- Happiness

As a rule of thumb I'm going to suggest the following. When your clients walk into your pitch they will naturally be in a state of curiosity about your solution; build on this emotional state. You want them interested in what you have to say and you want them to be in a state of anticipation about the solution you have to offer. In addition, as you talk about their company you will probably fire off a state of pride in them as well. All of these emotions are useful.

During the middle of your pitch you want your clients excited by your offer and interested to hear more. There's also a good chance they will be relieved because you are solving a challenge for them. By the end of your pitch you want your clients happy and excited by what they can achieve, and committed to you. When you do this, they will feel like they have made the best choice by hiring you.

Of course, there might be times during your pitch when you need to talk about problems or areas of concern for your client. If you do, my preference is that you don't dwell on them too long. Instead, focus on how you can solve them. The more you talk about problems, the more stuck your client becomes in their problems. This means that you're putting them into and holding them in a negative emotional state. The key is not to depress you clients, but to get them excited about their future.

Ordering your content for maximum impact

Understand important need bit I you to it's this.

Getting things in the wrong sequence can be very confusing – and that was just a short sentence. Imagine how much information you need to convey in your pitch. It only takes a little bit of that information to be in the wrong place and you could really frustrate or confuse your client and risk losing their attention (and their business) altogether.

A simple way to structure your content is to imagine your entire pitch as a bridge. At one end is your client right now. What do they know? What do they believe about themselves? What's important to them? What are their challenges and concerns? At the other end of the bridge are the results they want to produce. Their personal and brand objectives. The middle of your bridge is made up of the individual sections that represent your solution.

When you put your client at either end of the bridge, your solution represents the path to your client's success. Typically, people say that the end of the bridge is about what you want your client to do, buy your product or service for example. Well, yes it is, but that focuses on what you want, not on your clients and what they want. If you want to keep your pitch on track, I recommend you stay focused on what the client wants; on their results.

The object of your pitch is to help your clients believe that they can produce the results they want. When you do this, you are influencing their logical decisions (see the Hierarchy of Influence) in your favour. Each section of your bridge should work towards this goal. The ideas in this book have been designed to help you to achieve this, but if you do nothing else, here are the key ideas. Have a logical solution your clients can understand and believe in. Keep them in a positive emotional state, which helps them see their future in a more positive way. Neutralise their limiting beliefs, so that they can see there is another, better way to look at things that concern them. Giving lots of detail and using testimonials are an effective way of demonstrating that what your clients want is possible, and that you can help them achieve it, because you have done it before. Also, you want to paint vivid pictures in your client's mind, when you talk about the opportunities that are waiting for them. Get them excited about their future. Once you start to combine these ideas with other ideas in this book, you will create a powerful belief within your client, about their ability to achieve their goals.

There are two useful techniques which will help you to construct the middle sections of your bridge. The first technique is the *4MAT System*, which will help you to structure your content. The second technique, Pacing and Leading, will help you to put the sections of your bridge, in the correct order.

Of course I can't tell you what content you should put in or leave out of your pitch, only you can do that. My suggestion, if asked, is that you get everything you think is relevant to your client and stick it up on a wall. Now, stand back and look at what you have. Then put yourself in your client's shoes. Think about their situation, about what's going on for them, their company, the type of people they are, their challenges, what they believe can be achieved and their goals in six months, a year, two years etc. Really look at your content from your client's point of view. Then ask yourself: "If I were the client, what are the key pieces of logical and emotional information I would need to know, to believe that I could have what I want?" Then start to cut down your content.

Once you have cut your content down, it's time to start structuring it using the *4MAT System*.

Using the 4MAT System to structure your content

The *4MAT System*[1], developed by Bernice McCarthy in the 1970s, helps you to structure your content in a way that will allow you to meet everyone's learning style.

When we learn new information, we all have specific questions that we need answered, to understand and process the information we're being given. Bernice McCarthy's study concluded that the questions we naturally ask fell into four main categories. When you use the *4MAT System* to structure your content, it allows you to present information to your clients, in a way that meets these four categories of questions and therefore everyone's learning style. Studies have shown that using the *4MAT System* improves retention and comprehension of all types of information.

Here are the four ways we all learn;

1. Why Learners.   35% of people.
2. What Learners.   22% of people.
3. How Learners.   18% of people.
4. What if Learners.   25% of people.

Although we all learn in all of the four ways, we tend to favour one way of learning. If you don't use the *4MAT*

System when delivering information, you will only be communicating with your client using your own learning style, which may not necessarily be theirs! A lot of pitches I've witnessed seem to be based around the "What" and "How" formats – this is what we have (the solution) and this is how we apply it. This is missing over 50% of the way people learn information, and that includes your clients.

So who are Why, What, How and What If Learners?

Why Learners: These are learners who seek meaning. Their key question is Why? You have to know and give the reasons why they should be listening to you and you have to do this first. Why learners will ask: "Why am I here?", "Why are you telling me this?" If you start your pitch with: "We have a great way of finding you more customers", everybody – but especially the Why Learners – think: "Great, I'm interested and I'm ready to know more". A good "Why" sets up your entire pitch.

If you look back at just this section, you will see that I started with a very small **"What"**, and then moved straight into the **"Why"**. There are two ways of satisfying the **Why** Learners. Firstly, by giving them a benefit statement (it meets everyone's learning style and improves retention) or, secondly, you can ask an engaging question related to the topic, such as: "How would you like to know how to meet everyone's learning style so your communication will be much more effective?"

After you have given the reasons why people need to listen, you then need to explain what you are talking about.

What Learners: These are analytical learners who are interested in knowledge. Their key question is, **What**? "What are you telling them about?" **What** learners are the note-takers. They want to know the facts and details, like "Where did the *4MAT System* come from?" and "What do the experts think about this?"

Again, if you look back over this section, the What is: The *4MAT System* was developed by Bernice McCarthy, it covers four learning styles. Here are the statistics for each style; here are what the learning styles need to know, etc.

You need to anticipate questions and incorporate the answers into your content at the appropriate points.

Then you need to satisfy the **How** learners.

How Learners: These are common sense learners who need to know how to apply your ideas. Their key question is, **How**? They will test what you have told them because they learn best by using their common sense, experimenting and trying things out for themselves. They are the experiential learners.

And finally we have the **What If Learners:** They are dynamic learners. Their question is, **What If**? They learn by exploration and self-discovery and want to know the future consequences of doing what you're suggesting. What results could they expect from you? What are the benefits of your proposal? They may well have questions about your pitch. They will want to know things like, "If we can use your service here, can we use it over there as well?" Many companies make time at the end of their pitch for questions. This meets the **What If** learners' learning style, because they are looking for new or hidden possibilities.

Here's what the *4MAT System* looks like in summary:

- Why – why are you telling your clients about this section, what's in it for them?
- What – what are you telling them about?
- How – how do they apply these ideas you have outlined in this section?
- What if – what are the benefits to your clients of applying your ideas.

Each section of your bridge needs to apply the *4MAT System*. If you have individual sections of your pitch that deal with marketing, procurement, taking over from a current supplier etc, you need to make sure you run through the *4MAT System* for each section. In exactly the same way I have done for each new topic in this book.

Another interesting point about the *4MAT System* is that it naturally ensures that you are delivering information in big picture, conceptual terms as well as giving the details. Your audience will most likely be a combination of people who need the big picture concepts and detail. The **Why** information tends to be big picture because you're outlining concepts. The **What** and **How** information tends to provide the details your clients need to understand your solution.

At the start of Part Two, we looked at some useful emotional states to take your clients through during your pitch. At the beginning of your pitch, I suggested you needed to create curiosity, anticipation and interest. Giving the **Why** upfront allows you to do this. Similarly the **What** and **How** are likely to provide relief and excitement about your offer. Finally, commitment comes from seeing the results you're able to produce for your clients, the benefits to them, the **What if** and by having their questions answered at the end of your pitch.

So, now that you know how to structure your content to meet everyone's learning styles, let's look at how you can order the sections of your bridge to avoid confusion.

Using Pacing and Leading in your pitch

I've already said that Pacing and Leading is a useful tool to help you order the sections of your bridge. That's because it allows you to work from within your client's point of view, in a way that makes it easy for them to accept new information.

When ordering the sections of your bridge, you need to start by talking about something your client is familiar with, and then add new information to what they already know. This way you're building from a position of familiarity. If the information you present jumps or is too much of a logical leap for your clients to make, you will confuse them, or lose them altogether.

Your Pacing statements are based upon the information you've gained from your basic and advanced questions, or the brief. This is all information that represents your client's point of view. Leading statements are any new information you have to offer as part of your solution. In your pitch, you're going to start by presenting information your clients are familiar with (pacing statements) and then offer them your solution (lead). When you use Pacing and Leading, you will find that you can move your clients more easily across your bridge, and that they will have less resistance to your ideas.

There is a rule-of-thumb to help you construct the sections of your bridge:

- Pace, pace, pace, lead – beginning of your presentation
- Pace, pace, lead, lead – middle of your presentation
- Pace, lead, lead, lead – middle of your presentation
- Lead, lead, lead, lead – end of your presentation

If you start your pitch by talking about things your client understands and is comfortable with, they are much more likely to be relaxed and engaged because they are in familiar territory. If you want to introduce new ideas at the beginning of the bridge, don't go too fast, keep coming back to "touch base" by pacing them again. Familiar information acts like a handrail, steadying them across. As you get towards the middle and end of your bridge, you will naturally be adding larger and larger chunks of new information (Leading), as the client's confidence in you and your solution grows.

I did this in Part One. I started with something you knew, basic questions and rapport, and then moved on to something that was new to you (eliciting and working with values and beliefs). As I added more information, I went slowly so I knew you understood what I was talking about.

As well as helping you order the sections of your bridge, Pacing and Leading is also an extremely powerful linguistic tool. As I have hinted, Pacing and Leading allows you to gain agreement to the suggestions you're making. This happens because you're going to tell your clients things that they know to be true and therefore agree with (Pacing), then you add a suggestion (Lead) which you want them to believe is true and therefore also agree with.

When you use Pacing and Leading linguistically, you're offering three statements which are absolutely true, followed by a suggestion that you want your client to take onboard as being true.

As you hold this book, reading through this material, letting your eyes skim the words, you may find that new ideas pop into your mind about how you can win more pitches. In this example, holding the book, reading the material and skimming the words are all Pacing statements. They are all undeniably true. The Lead, suggestion, is finding new ideas and winning more pitches.

This technique works because the "critical factor"[2], the part of your brain that rejects information it doesn't believe in, gets bored of agreeing with your true statements, and basically goes "offline". Three examples of true information are usually enough for the critical factor to go "offline". The fourth, the Lead, therefore bypasses the critical factor to be accepted as true. As a note, in the example above, when I gave you the Lead, about ideas popping into your mind, I didn't say they would definitely happen. I said "you *may* find that ideas pop into your mind..." Your Pacing statements have to be irrefutably true statements of fact for your clients. However, your Leading statement will be more easily accepted if it refers to the possibility of something happening, rather than it definitely happening. This means you want to use words like, may, could, might and should for your Leading statement. As opposed to words like will and must.

Now you know about the "critical factor", I need to mention one more thing about the bridge again. You see, when you build your bridge based upon what your client already knows (Pacing statements), you are in effect sending their critical factor "offline" and this is what reduces resistance to the solution you're offering (Leading statements).

There are a number of linguistic Pacing and Leading statements you can make. You can Pace and Lead your client's actual experience, at that moment. I did this in my example earlier about reading this book. The other type of Pacing and Leading which might be useful is Pacing and Leading your client's point of view or experience.

Let's say you know your client has another supplier, and that you know roughly how much they spent with that supplier and what results that supplier has produced for them. Your Pacing statements would be:

"When you where with supplier X, they were able to produce result Y for you, which is actually a fairly healthy return on your initial investment of Z."

As the client knows all of these statements to be true, their critical factor starts to go "offline". Now you add your Lead:

"And during our presentation, we would like to show you how we believe you might be able to increase your result Y by more than 5% over the next two years."

Your 5% increase is far more likely to be accepted as true when it's presented as part of a Pace and Lead.

Summary

- There are useful emotions to use in your pitch which will help to keep your client engaged and interested.

- Think of your pitch as a bridge and put your clients at either end of it.

- Your content has to help your clients believe they can have what they most want. Only put in what you need to achieve this.

- The *4MAT System* allows you to meet everyone's learning style and improves your client's ability to retain the information you present to them.

- Use the *4MAT System* to structure each individual section of content.

- You have to order your content in the following way. Why, What, How and What If.

- In the Why give big picture and concepts. What and How are about detail. What If can be detail or big picture. The What If is either your benefit slide at the end of each section, or questions at the end of your pitch.

- Pacing and Leading allows you to order the sections of your bridge.

- It builds information from a position of familiarity and helps your logic flow.

- The rule at the beginning of your bridge is; Pace, Pace, Pace, Lead.

- Towards the middle and end of your bridge, you will naturally be Leading your clients much more.

- Pacing and Leading is also a powerful linguistic tool.

- Give three true statements and then your suggestion. This allows your suggestion to bypass your client's critical factor.

Exercises

- As you design your pitch, try to engage your client using positive learning states.
- To build your bridge, find a blank wall and stick up all the information you have about your client's current challenges, concerns, beliefs and values etc. A few feet away, stick up all the information you have about the results they want to produce.
- In the middle, stick up all the information you have that could help them reach their objective.
- Cut down your content to the information your clients need to believe that they can produce the results they want. Put yourself in their shoes to do this.
- Run through the *4MAT System* to structure your content. Why, What, How and What If.
- Use Pacing and Leading to order the sections of your bridge.

As we come to the end of this section, please rate how much more persuasive you believe you could be in your next pitch, as a result of the information you now have. Please write your percentage improvement score below.

| %|

2.
SPEAKING THE SAME LANGUAGE AS YOUR CLIENT

Bringing your pitch alive in the minds of your audience (with Visual, Auditory, Emotional and Logical Language)

FOR THOSE OF YOU WHO know about NLP, in this section I'm going to use slightly different terminology than you might normally expect to see, such as referring to Representational System as language types, replacing kinaesthetic with emotion and Audio Digital with logic. I'm doing this to simplify the terminology.

So, how would you like to bring your pitch to life in the minds of your audience? To really engage with them much more deeply? One way to do this is to speak the same language as they do.

I don't mean when you go to France, you speak French. I'm talking about using the same words and phrases as your clients do. In effect, you're building rapport with your clients by mirroring their own language. This builds greater trust and reassures them about you.

So what kind of words or phrases do you look out for when you're talking to someone? And, therefore, what kind of words or phrases might you want to feed back to your clients to build rapport?

The words and phrases we need to look out for are split into four different types. These types are, visual words or phrases, auditory words or phrases, emotional words or phrases and logical words or phrases.

When people speak to you, they will either be using one of these four types of language, or a combination. All you need to do is listen out for their preferred language type and adjust your language to match theirs (if you are using a different language type).

Let me give you an example to demonstrate how useful this concept is. A couple of years ago a client, Giles, came to see me because he was having trouble communicating with his sister, Beth. In fact, over the last few years, their relationship had gone from bad to almost not speaking at all. When they did speak it invariably ended in an argument. It had got so bad that any communication was now limited to letters but even this form of communication was getting progressively more difficult. Giles was concerned that his sister had lost her job and hadn't managed to find another one. Knowing that Beth had limited savings, Giles was keen to help her find a new job.

When I visited the Giles, we talked about what was going on and it quickly became apparent that he was very logical. I looked at the letters he had written to his sister. He was only trying to give her sensible advice which was meant to help. Everything he said was completely logical and made sense. Then he showed me the responses he had received from his sister. Beth was angry and cross because she felt he was blaming her for her predicament and not helping. It was very apparent that Beth was using emotional language. I suggested that to improve the relationship, Giles was going to have to write to his sister using emotional language. He was going to communicate with her by mirroring back the emotional words she had used in her letters and encourage her to help herself. Giles wrote the letter and within a week received a reply. Beth finally felt that Giles understood her and the relationship started to improve. In fact, things took a dramatic turn for the better, to the point where phone conversations could now be held without things turning ugly. With some "emotional" help from Giles, Beth found a new job which she is very happy in. Of course, Giles needs to keep up the emotional language every time he communicates with Beth, but for him it was a real breakthrough because he was able to help Beth and give her advice in a way that she could accept and understand.

This experience illustrates the need to work within your client's language type. I described this miscommunication as like speaking a different language, and that's really what it is. Beth was describing her world using emotions, and Giles described his world using logic. The way they each describe their world is the way they see it. Their miscommunication, which started out with them not understanding each other, ultimately resulted in a breakdown in trust. Of course, other factors were at play, but when Giles became more emotional in his communication, it had a dramatic impact on their relationship.

During the pitch process, start listening for what language types your clients are using. Is it logical language, emotional language, auditory language or visual language? If you can determine which of these four language types they're using, you can match their language and feed it back to them. This will help you to fit very closely into the way they see their world. The more you see the world in the same way, the more rapport you build and the more persuasive you become.

Before we go into a description of each of the language types and how you can recognise them in your clients, colleagues and friends, I need to point out that it would be very unusual for a person to stay in the same language type all the time. In the story above, when I talked to the Giles about Beth and what was going on, he became upset and his language switched from logical to become much more emotional. Like Giles, I use very logical language, but if you talk to me about my family I will switch to emotional language. This means that the language types we use are context specific. So to improve your communication with your clients, you need to be aware of when they are switching between the language types and, if you can, follow their lead and switch too.

Here are the language types and the characteristics that people display:

Visual people

These are people who describe their world using pictures.

Physical characteristics: They stand upright. They breathe high in their chests. They will often look up to the right or left during a conversation, this is to recall a visual memory or create a visual picture. Visual people speak quickly because visual memories are quicker and more easily accessed. In the section on building rapport over the phone, I talked about matching the speed at which people speak. If you speak quickly, you are also matching a visual person's communications style.

Language: Visual people describe their world using visual language. They talk in terms of how things look. They use words like: see, clear, look, bright, dim, focused, reveal, hazy, foggy, appear. They use phrases like, it appears to me, I take a dim view on that, looks like a bright idea, in view of, see to it, short sighted, beyond a shadow of a doubt.

The way something looks can have a dramatic impact on the way a visual person responds to you. Something that happened to me a while back: I gave a client my business card, they said that the typeface was too small and that they didn't like the colour of the card. Then they used my card to wipe some fluff off their trousers! I knew from their comments that they were visual, but this took me by surprise. Having used my card as a scraper, it was pretty clear they weren't going to work with me.

Auditory people

These are people who describe their world using sound.

Physical characteristics: They tend to stand upright. They tend to breathe in the middle of their chests. They tend to speak clearly and at an even pace, as well as having good pronunciation, because being understood is very important to them. They look straight across, to the left or right during a conversation, to access an auditory memory or to create a sound.

Language: Auditory people use the way things sound to them to describe their world. They use words like: listen, hear, resonate, tune in/out, rings a bell, silence, quiet, announce. They use phrases like: that sounds like a good idea, I hear what you're saying, it's as clear as a bell, tongue-tied, voice an opinion, word for word.

The way something sounds has a big effect on an auditory person. If you mumble or don't speak clearly, they can lose interest in what you're saying relatively quickly. A simple way to tell if someone is auditory is to notice if they get distracted by ambient sounds, like other people talking or noises they can't control. This is something you need to be very aware of in your pitch. It's another good reason to avoid talking over each other during your pitch, and it will be really distracting for them if there are building works or loud road works going on.

Emotional people

These are people who experience the world through both the way they feel emotionally and also how something feels to them when they touch it or experience it (easy or difficult and hot or cold). A simplistic way to describe emotional people is to say that they are ruled by their heart.

Physical characteristics: Emotional people tend to stoop. They breathe from their stomachs. They speak slowly, because it takes time to feel the emotions they want to express. They look down and to the left (as you look at them), to access emotions during a conversation.

Language: Emotional people talk about how they feel. They will use words that express emotions like: happy, sad, confident, lost, frustrated, elated. They also use words that express ideas around touching things like: grasp, feel, touch, hot, cold, rough, smooth. They use phrases like: I love that film, I'm so happy, can you grasp this, they're a bit hot headed, hold on, get a grip.

The way you make emotional people feel about you will have a great impact on your relationship with them, or even if they will work with you or not. It's my experience that emotional people tend to hold onto emotions longer than other types. Also, emotional people will be aware of the room temperature, how comfortable a chair is, whether they are under any pressure, etc.

Logical people

These are people who are interested in logic, criteria and benefits. They like order and tend to have a lot of internal dialogue. If emotional people are ruled by their hearts, then logical people are ruled by their heads.

Physical characteristics: Like emotional people, logical people tend to have poor posture. They breathe from their stomachs. They can speak slowly, but not always because their speech rate is determined by their next most dominant language type. They look down and to the right (as you look at them) to access their internal dialogue.

Language: Logical people use language like: understand, learn, think, know, process, conceive, decide. They use phrases like: I think I understand, I know what you mean, you won't change my thinking, it's all in the process, can you outline the steps.

Logic, criteria and benefits are the most important things to a logical person. They need to understand things. Typically, a logical person will wake up in the middle of the night and have trouble getting back to sleep because they have lots of internal dialogue going on. They might be making lists in their head about things to do, or solving problems. During the day, logical people can often seem distant or disconnected from conversations or gatherings because they are processing information and talking to themselves about what's going on.

Now that you are familiar with the language types, let's look at how you might present information to each of them.

There are a number of well-known car shows in the UK. In these shows, when the presenters test-drive a car, they talk about how the car looks, its lines, whether it looks cool or not, what colours it comes in, what the engine sounds like, whether they like the sound of it or not. Many times they will get excited about how wonderful it sounds and use descriptive language to express the roar of the engine. During the test-drive they'll tell you how comfortable it is, how it handles, or even how it makes them feel. They also give you the spec. How fast it goes, how big the engine is, the top speed, the 0-60 time, the torque and the MPG. Do they talk about these things by accident? I think they do it to meet everyone's language type, to make sure they are communicating with everyone who's watching. So that everyone enjoys the show. If they didn't, if they only told you about what it was like to drive and the engine noise, they would be missing out the people who want to know the facts and figures, and the people who want to know about how it looks, what colours it comes in etc.

Now you have an idea of what types of language people use to communicate, the question is what is your preferred language type? There are a number of free online tests you can do: just type "free representational system tests" into your favourite search engine and one will come up. It is worth doing the test to see if you are what you think you are.

If you've done the test, then now you know what your preferred language type is. Obviously, I don't know which test you have done, but here are a couple of points which will probably apply to your results. Some of you might find that your preference leans much more towards one language type than the others. This is what I have. I'm very logical. This meant that for me, communicating in emotional, visual and auditory language was something I had to think about. In fact, I had to practise at the start, because it didn't always come that easily for me. If, on the other hand you are fairly evenly spread between the different language types, this means that you can switch more easily between them.

Now you know what language type you are, it's time to look at how you can communicate using someone else's language type. I'm going to tell the story from each language type's point of view.

It's a story about a little dog sitting by the road.

You know those really bright sunny days, where everything looks really vibrant? Well, it was one of those days and I was walking down the road when I saw this cool little dog. It was one of those dogs with a white, wiry coat. As I got closer to it, I could tell that it was looking at something across the road. When I looked, I could see that he had spotted some sausages in a butchers shop. They were just hanging from a hook in the window, dangling there. I could almost see the dog drooling as he watched the sausages very closely. Suddenly, he ran out into the road; he didn't look, he just ran straight for the sausages. Then I noticed a big car, heading down the road towards the dog. I couldn't see how the dog was going to make it. The driver of the car didn't look like he was paying any attention to the road. The dog just kept running right into the path of the oncoming car. Then the dog noticed the car too. Suddenly, and I'm still not sure how he did it, but he managed to just avoid the car's bumper by only inches. Anyway, the dog got to the other side of the road and the last thing I saw was him disappearing into the butchers shop.

Hopefully, you can see that the above description is seen through a visual point of view.

Here's another one:

Have you noticed how loud those jackhammers are, that workmen use by the side of the road? They have to wear the ear protectors because it's so darn noisy and you can't even hear yourself think when you walk past them. Anyway, I was walking down the noisiest street in our town, when I noticed a little dog, one of those that don't have a big dog bark, more of a yap. He was sitting there by the side of the road, good as gold. Not a peep. Then suddenly, there was a yap and he was off. Straight across the road, out he ran. Out in front of a car. He was clearly after something on the other side of the road. Now I was expecting the blast of a horn to warn this dog, but nothing; the car just kept on going. There was not even a squeal of breaks. I was about to shout when, and I don't know how he managed to do it, the dog got clear of the car and ended up outside a butchers. He was panting pretty hard I can tell you.

I'm telling these stories in a way that makes the language type pretty obvious. Just so we're clear, when you listen to people they might not always be this obvious.

Here's another one:

What a lovely day. The sun was beating down and I could feel its warmth on my back as I walked down the street. I was just enjoying the moment, when I noticed one of these really cute little doggies. The ones that are like a big, furry, snowball. I love those dogs. Something across the road had his attention. Then, suddenly he was off as fast as his legs would carry him. Then, oh my, there was this great big car heading right for him. Forget the dog, my heart was racing, let alone his. I was really worried for him. I started to run towards him to help, just in case something happened. Just when I thought that little dog would be, well you know, going to heaven, he managed to make it to the other side. I was so relieved and you know what, that driver didn't even care, he would have only known he had hit that cute little dog, if he felt a thud. Drivers like that make me mad.

Are you getting the feel for this now? I know it won't be long before you'll be confidently using all of these language types.

Here's the final one:

I was just thinking to myself how things were going at work, when this dog, from nowhere, suddenly ran out into the road. Now, the road was pretty wide, and there was this big car and I mean big. The wheels on this thing must have been at least twelve inches wide and they had those low profile tyres as well. It was a race. Could the dog make it far enough across the road before the wheels got to him? From where I was standing, I thought: "No way, it's impossible". There just wasn't time and the dog wasn't going fast enough. But, and I don't know how, he got across the road in the nick of time. Thinking about it, there's no way that dog should have been able to make it across the road, but he did. I remember saying to myself as I walked away, that dog must have nine lives too.

Hopefully by now, you should be able to understand how these language types are working and what benefits you could get from using them.

Let's contextualise this in more detail, by looking at one of the most common forms of communication. The following examples are based on actual emails. As you read them, think about what language type the person is using to communicate and therefore, how you would use this language type back to them to improve your communication with them.

First example:

> Marcus will position the content for the training. He'll write it up and let Ian add his thoughts. Marcus can structure the day to produce the results we want.
>
> Regards,

Second example:

> It would be great to catch up, let me know when you're around. I wish I had fantastic clients! If you ever need a hand, I would be happy to help!

Third example:

> Trouble's looming. Can you two please take a look at this!

Fourth example:

> Will ask around for sure. It sounds like a good talk, so will be more than happy to recommend it.
>
> Speak soon

Fifth example:

> I will aim to get back to you later this afternoon with some proposed dates as suggested, to move things forward. I'm still playing "juggle the diary" with a few clients concerning the next few weeks but should have some visibility by close of play.

Hopefully, examples one to four are now pretty straightforward and it's likely that the people sending these emails had a strong preference towards one of the four language types, but looking at this last example, it might not be immediately clear which language type the person is. When you come across this, you want to look at the context and what language type they have used in that context. Looking at the email above, I would say that at the start of this email, the sender is using logical language (*some proposed dates as suggested*). When they reference their diary, they talk about juggling it. To me this is emotional language. It's about trying to get a hold of the clients, grasping at them and even slight frustration. Finally, the sender talks about having some visibility, which is clearly visual language.

So when you reply to this person, you want to use logical language to talk about the proposed dates, emotion when you want to talk about clients and visual language to talk about getting something to them.

Here's an example of what I mean:

> Let me know when you can about the proposed dates, obviously we want to move everything forward as soon as possible, but I understand that clients can be hard to pin down to anything that looks like a commitment.

In this example I have mirrored the emails structure, proposed dates, clients and close of play. I have also mirrored the emails language. All I did was look at the language type in context, and then feed it back to the sender.

A final note about emails, a good clue to the sender's language type is to look at how they sign off their emails. Do they use:

- Love – emotional.
- Speak soon – auditory.
- Best – emotional.
- Regards – logical.
- Cheers – emotional/auditory.
- Kind regards – emotional/logical.
- Thanks – emotional (but less than thank you).
- Best wishes – emotional.
- Thank you – emotional.
- Many thanks – emotional.
- Catch up soon – emotional.
- See you soon – visual.

As a rule, I always like to mirror the client's signoff back to them. Even if I get everything else wrong, I do this, because this is about how they want to be seen and remembered by me, as well as being a reflection of their preferred language type.

In cases where I initiate the email, if I know someone is visual I will use a visual signoff. If they are auditory, I use an auditory signoff and so on.

You can use your signoff in other ways as well. I use some signoffs as a call to action. I often use, "speak soon" when I'm going to call someone or want them to call me or when I want them to take some action for me. By putting "speak soon", it implies that contact will be made soon, so you might want to do something about what I'm talking about in the email. This is subtle stuff and it doesn't guarantee success all the time, but it is something to think about. Similarly, "see you soon", implies the same thing. I use "kind regards", because I'm predominantly logical. I also use it a lot because of the business environment I work in.

So, when you first start to interact with clients, even before your pre-pitch meeting, you need to be looking at the language types they are using and the context they are using it in. If you can start building rapport from the very first point of contact, it will help develop a deeper and more persuasive relationship.

In addition to your emails, you need to pepper all of your communication with visual, auditory, logical and emotional language. Any documentation you send across to your clients, any questions or answers to their questions, you either need to consider including all the language types, or you need to look at their preferred language type and feed it back to them. As a guide, if your emails, documents or slides are going to be read by more than a few people, you need to use all the language types.

This is relatively easy to do, if you are aware of it. However, if like me, you have a strong preferred language type, you need to bear in mind that you will probably write your documents around this language type. All you have to do is take extra care to make sure you include the three other language types. If you really can't manage it, find someone in your company who has an equally strong but different language type to yours, and get them to go through the document when you have finished. You need to keep using all four language types once you have started because, if you start and then suddenly stop, at an unconscious level your clients will notice that something has changed and this could then start to work against you. Keep building rapport and trust with them.

Finally, Let's look at how you apply this information to the actual pitch. In a pitch, when you speak, you will predominantly use your own language type. There's nothing wrong with this, it's perfectly natural. Again, if you can, try to include the other language types. It's actually easier than you think. Here's something I might say to cover all the language types when I start a new training session with my clients.

"Good morning, how's everyone doing? Over the next two days I'm going to tell you about some simple yet powerful ideas that can help you to win more pitches. What I want you to do as we talk through these ideas is think about all the ways you could start to apply these concepts to your next pitch. So that, by the end of the training, you'll be able to clearly see the benefits of being here."

Go back and read this again and look at the order I've run through. I've covered everything, but it sounds quite normal. Here's the breakdown: Emotional: "How's everyone doing?" Auditory: "to tell you about… talk through these…" Logical: "these ideas, is think about, benefits of…" Visual: "clearly see…".

Now, you might not want to have to remember to say this, or something similar, in your pitch. Or you might be thinking, well I'm logical and I have colleagues who are visual and emotional and they are presenting as well, so that covers it. And you're right, it probably would, but you really want to get everyone engaged as soon as possible because it will be more beneficial to your pitch. So the first person needs to run through all of the language types at the start of your pitch, rather than waiting for a colleague to engage the emotional people forty-five minutes in.

Here's a simple workaround. If you remember, I told you that different language types speak at different speeds. Therefore to build rapport with emotional people you have to speak slowly, to build rapport the auditory people you need to speak at an even pace and to build rapport with visual people you need to speak quickly. If you listen to great speakers, they vary the speed at which they speak, which, as well as a way to build rapport, makes it much more interesting to listen to.

So, if you're the first presenter in your pitch to stand up, I'm going to recommend you start off by speaking slowly. Then, over the first few minutes, slowly speed up to a more even paced speed, which will build rapport with auditory people. Finally, you want to be speaking quickly, to build rapport with the visual people. Once you have spoken quickly for a minute or so, slow down to your normal speed. That way you include all the language types in your presentation without having to remember to use; visual, auditory, emotional and logical language.

Here are a couple of tricks you can do by varying the rate at which you speak. During your pitch there might be some areas of concern for the client. If you don't want to highlight these concerns, keep speaking at your normal speed or even a little faster. Remember, it takes time for emotions to build. If you slow down there's a good chance you will allow your clients to get emotionally engaged in their concerns. Similarly, when you get to parts of your pitch that are good news, you need to have excitement in your voice, and to slow down a little to let the good news sink in. To give your good news more importance and prominence, put pauses in. Pauses are like putting a full stop in your sentence and it gives your clients time to take in your point. If I told you I could double your profits, but didn't give you a chance to get excited about it, you would feel a little cheated. In fact, you might question whether I really could produce those results for you.

Another thing to notice in a pitch is that you usually use your preferred language type to ask and answer questions. It's the difference between: "Would you like to ask us anything? "Now you've seen our proposal, is everything clear? "We know you probably have some questions, at this point... "We have a feeling you might have some questions". Ask yourself what your client's preferred language type is and reflect on whether you are asking and answering the questions in their language type. If you answer a question using visual language and your client is logical, they might feel that you haven't answered the question to their satisfaction. This is why the pre-pitch meetings are so important. Listen out for preferred language types, who is using what? If key players have a real preference for one language type, use it when answering questions for them. Help them to feel good about your pitch.

Another thing you can do, which I do in training sessions if I'm running out of time, is to ask a question without using a questioning tonality. This limits the number of questions I receive, sometimes to no questions at all. A questioning tonality rises up at the end of the sentence. Australians are great examples of people who have a questioning tonality. When you first start to take questions at the end of your pitch, use the questioning tonality. Then, when you want to start limiting the questions, start to change your tonality. Instead of going up at the end of the sentence, keep your tone even. Then when you really don't want any more questions, drop your tone at the end of the sentence. Instead of saying: "Do you have any questions?" change to: "Is there anything else?"

Finally, before we leave this section, I wanted to tell you about a concept I have been thinking about. It takes the concepts of language types a little further. Let me start by saying this: I believe that when people are criticised and they react strongly to that criticism, it's because it criticises their self-image. For example, if you see yourself as funny and someone points out how terrible your jokes are, you might really take it to heart. It stands to reason then, if you want to build greater rapport with people you need to flatter the image they have of themselves. What they say about themselves will tell you a lot about how they see themselves. In addition to flattering their self-image in a conversation, why not flatter their self-image using their own language type? Visual people, tend to spend a lot of time and effort on the way things look, why not flatter them on how they look, or the look of their presentation, or the care they have taken over the font or the colours? Talk about how the thing that they care about most had a positive effect on the client or the people around them. Do this sincerely, don't just say it for fun, people can tell when you're not being genuine. Similarly, with auditory people: you tell them how their clarity has really helped a situation. How their talk was really clear and resonated with the client. Use their language to flatter them about their language type. Emotional people need to hear how their feelings were helpful to others and how others could grasp the concepts more easily as a result. Logical people need to hear how their logic has really helped the situation, how they helped the client to understand the concepts more effectively. Think about how you could use this idea to great effect, it's the opposite of a criticism and it will make the people around you feel great. How might your clients react to this if you were to flatter them in their language type too?

Summary
- There are four different language types. Visual, Auditory, Emotional and Logical.
- We all use all four language types, but most people have a preference for one.
- We switch between language types depending on the context of the conversation.
- Communicating with your clients in their language type, means you are building rapport and therefore your communication will resonate more powerfully with them.
- In any communication with more than three clients, written or verbal, you need to use each of the four language types.

- Each language type uses its own words and phrases.
- Visual people speak quickly, auditory people speak at an even pace, and emotional people tend to speak slowly.
- You can replicate the language types in your pitch, by varying the speed at which you speak.
- Match your client's language type in emails.
- Flattering people in their own language type will have a positive impact on them.

Exercises

- Start to listen out for what language types your friends, colleagues and clients are using.
- Practise speaking in a different language type, choose one you're not familiar with. For example, if you could only describe the world using pictures, how would you describe it?
- Get used to listening out for changes in language types during a conversation; this will happen when the context of the conversation changes.
- Look at the emails you send and receive, start to match the sender's language type. Especially their sign off.
- Make a conscious effort to listen out for, and then use, different language types during a conversation.

3.
THE CRYSTAL BALL APPROACH

How to understand where your clients are emotionally when structuring your content, not during the pitch

By understanding your client's emotional state as you design your presentation, you're making sure everyone is continually engaged during your actual pitch. You don't want to leave key clients out in the cold for long periods of time, because they may well drift off, which means they aren't going to be focusing on you and what you're saying.

At the end of each section of your bridge, ask yourself these questions:

1. Who has just had all the attention?
2. Who haven't we connected with recently?
3. How much do the individuals believe they can have what they want?
4. What emotions are the key decision makers feeling?

You might have noticed that at the end of certain sections, I ask you how much more persuasive you believe you are now? It's the same thing.

If someone has been left out, you need to re-engage them. Only you will be able to determine the best way to do this. However, if you think about how your clients might be feeling as you structure your bridge, you stand a much greater chance of keeping them engaged and enjoying your pitch than you would by winging it in the pitch.

Another thing to consider is that sometimes it can be helpful to let a key client have a little time to digest what you have said, rather than piling more information onto them. If you overload people they are just as likely to disengage as if you ignore them.

Summary
- It's easier and more productive to look at where you're clients are emotionally as you structure your content, rather than leaving it to chance in your pitch.
- To do this ask yourself, who have I engaged with, who hasn't had any attention, do the individuals believe they can produce the results they want, and what emotions are the key decision makers feeling?

Exercises
- What solutions do you have if you know you're going to create a negative emotion? Leave someone out? Or your clients aren't in a useful learning state?
- Be ruthless. Make the changes before you get to your pitch.

As we leave this section on gauging emotions in your pitch. I want you to rate how much more persuasive you believe you could be in your pitch, as a result of the information you now have. Please write your percentage improvement score below.

4.
CREATING A MORE PERSUASIVE BEGINNING, MIDDLE AND END

Structuring the beginning of your pitch

"WELCOME. MY NAME IS..."

You've introduced yourself and thanked your client for being there.

Now what?

Having a great introduction sets the tone for your entire pitch. Get it right and you really start to engage and build a bond of trust. Get it wrong and you can lose people and never get them back. Your introduction is where you get your clients interested and engaged in your pitch. In this chapter, we're going to look at some ideas you can use to build this interest and really engage your clients.

Having introduced yourself, there are two things you can do.

1. Establish your credentials

Not every company establishes their credentials in their pitch. Some industries require it and love it, and some don't. But if you do, here are some thoughts you might like to consider.

Establishing your credentials is telling your client who you've worked with before and what you've done for them. You're offering your client the social proof (also see testimonials) that says how good you are. The logic is, if I'm good enough to help these people/companies, I'm good enough to help you. If I tell you I helped my clients make over twenty-five million pounds and I'm going to show you how you could do the same, I've got your attention.

For me, establishing your credentials in your introduction is like telling your client how brilliant you are, rather than demonstrating it. Once you do this, there's a chance that your client will sit there and think, "go on then, show me" and if they are thinking this during your pitch, they're not engaged in your solution. Instead they will be looking for examples of where you don't deliver on being brilliant and the more examples they can find, the more barriers come up.

If you really need to establish your credentials, I favour subtlety. I recommend that one of my clients used logos from all the companies they had worked at, in their opening slide. They had a great track record and therefore some great logos, and I knew this would help reassure their clients, but instead of making a big deal about it, I suggested that they say something along these lines: "This is the breadth of experience we can bring to your business." I suggested that they should hold on the slide for fifteen seconds so that the prospect sees lots of fantastic logos, then move on to the next slide to talk about how they could help the client. The client will think: "Wow, I get all this experience helping me," and because the presenter wouldn't be making a big deal about it, the client would want to know more. This gave them an opportunity during the questions to talk about who they had worked with, after they'd had a chance to prove themselves.

Another, subtle way to talk about company credentials is to do it when you introduce a colleague during the pitch. As you hand over to a colleague, point out how they achieved XYZ results (your credentials). In fact, a hand over is a great time to do lots of covert things. Like, linking your colleague to a client's value statement (question one of the Golden Questions). "This is Steve, he has helped many of our clients continually produce *sustainable results*." Or, as you introduce a colleague, point out how they have helped other clients produce the same supporting beliefs held by your client. Also, look at this from your colleague's point of view. If you are about to present and the person introducing you says how great you are, you're likely to feel pretty good about yourself, which will be reflected in your presentation. Helping your colleagues feel good about what they are about to present is a great way of helping nervous presenters feel a little more at ease.

The second thing you can do after you've introduced yourself, is tell your client how you can help them.

2. Let them know you have a solution for them

Let's be honest, that's why your clients are there.

So, you don't need to shy away from your solution. However, and this is important, your solution has to be realistic and believable for your clients. Remember, clients act in accordance with their beliefs. Pitches can be lost because clients don't believe you can produce the results you are claiming.

It's not my job to tell you how good or bad your solution is but it is my job to ask you if you think your client will believe it? Of course you can use pre-frames, metaphors and do all the things we have talked about, but at the start of your pitch you want your clients totally committed. So make sure the things you start with are easy for your clients to understand, commit to and believe in. Which brings us back to Pacing them.

When you outline your solution in the introduction, I'm going to recommend you talk about it in terms of concepts. Your introduction isn't about detail, it's only about big picture; concepts. You don't want to give detailed information in the introduction about how you'll achieve these results because, firstly, you need to have a hook that creates enough interest for your clients to engage in your pitch. If you give everything away, what else is there for your clients to engage with? Secondly, detailed information can introduce resistance and that's the last thing you want at the beginning of your pitch. Here's an example: If you tell your client that the best way to attract more customers is for them to invest in people handing out flyers at the point of sale, they might well reject the idea, but if you say: "We have a very exciting way of attracting new customers, which would increase your current customer base by..." they are going to get excited. This gives you the opportunity to explain during your pitch why handing out flyers will work so well.

I have found that percentages are a nice abstract way to talk about how much you can help your clients. They are abstract enough for your clients to understand them, without necessarily knowing what they mean in real terms, until you explain this later in your pitch. It's also useful, if you can, to try to have something in your introduction for the key decision makers. Hooking the individuals by telling them that there's something coming up for them, means that they become emotionally invested in how you are able to produce these results for them. If you were to say: "Our solution means that sales will be up by 20%," do you think the Sales Director would be engaged during your pitch for more information about his 20% increase? By only giving clients the big picture in the introduction, you're firing off two critical learning states, curiosity and interest. Of course, not every pitch is about growth or ROI and therefore you can't always talk about percentages. Advertising agencies, for example, focus on strategies and ideas. The key is to use your introduction to elicit useful emotional states and to create hooks that will keep your clients engaged during your pitch.

We've already looked at a number of ways to build these emotional hooks, but to recap, here's the list so far.

- Having a solution is an emotional hook.

- Building rapport, through understanding and empathising with your client, is another emotional hook.

- When you attach an individual's value statement to your pitch, which you could do as you handover to a colleague, it's a further emotional hook.

- If you have them wanting to know more about how you can help them, again it's an emotional hook.

All of these hooks working together help create a powerful emotional bond between you and your client and the more ways you can engage your client emotionally, the more persuasive you become and the more committed they become to you. It's about engaging clients emotionally as well as logically.

To that end, in the next section we will look at how you can use your introduction to set-up your hooks, Pacing and Leading statements, visual, auditory, emotional, logical language, introduce yourself, introduce others, and introduce pre-frames and your solution. Adapt it to your own style and use what you feel is most useful.

Summary

- Your introduction sets the tone for the rest of you pitch. As the saying goes: "First impressions count!"

- If you use your credentials at the beginning of your pitch, think about how they will be received by the client.

- I favour subtlety when showing credentials, like linking them to a colleague you're introducing. This way they don't get in the way of your pitch.

- Your client is there to hear your solution.

- Your solution has to hook your client emotionally. They have to want to know more from you.

- Your introduction should be about concepts not detail. Details can create resistance, and that's the last thing you need at the start of your pitch.

- Percentages are a good way of showing an increase without giving the numbers away.

Exercises

- Think about better, more interesting ways to present your credentials.

- What emotional hooks could you use?

Putting it All Together: Your Introduction

Welcome slide

"Good morning and welcome. As many of you know, my name is Marcus Corah and I'm CEO of our company. Firstly, I wanted to thank you all for being here today and giving us this opportunity to tell you about some of the ideas we have, that we believe could considerably improve your market share. We also believe that as we take you through our presentation you'll see that we have a practical and easy way to implement a growth solution for you.

"As you know from the meetings leading up to today, we have taken time to really understand the challenges you're currently facing. Almost more importantly, this understanding is also based upon where you want to be in three years from now and it's this that we want to focus on today: how we can best help you achieve these results. Our aim is to simply show you how you can achieve the growth you want."

Growth slide

"As you can see from this slide, we believe we can meet your future growth targets by focusing on two main areas. They are, targeting your current customers and helping you to find new customers. By improving your ability to attract and retain a higher share of your customers, we believe you could make significant increases in the overall growth of your business. In fact, we estimate that within a two-year period, you could see your sales grow by over 20%. But, that's not all. This forecasted growth is only part of the story, because we'll also explain how we can reduce the unit cost of acquiring new customers for you.

"Before we get into the details of how this can be achieved. I would like to take this opportunity to introduce John. John has worked for us for over four years, during which time he has won two industry awards, which has been an integral part of helping us to a top ten ranking. John..."

"Thank you. As we are all aware, the world we live in has changed considerably over the last few years and sometimes it seems to be happening more rapidly than we can reasonably keep up with. Whilst we are in the throes of change it can be easy to lose sight of the long-term objectives. So today, as Marcus has said, we want to focus on where you want to get to as a brand, not what might stop us from getting there. So let's start by..."

So, let's look at what we have done in this introduction.

Welcome Slide

"Good morning *(pacing statement, it is morning and emotional language – good)* and welcome *(emotional language)*. As many of you know, my name is Marcus Corah and I'm CEO of our company" *(pacing statement,*

I am called Marcus and I am CEO and they know this). Firstly, I wanted to thank you all for being here today *(pace, that's exactly what I am doing)* and giving us this opportunity to tell *(auditory language)* you about some of the ideas we have that we believe could considerably improve your market share *(pacing statement, this is why they are there and logical language).* We also believe that as we take you through our presentation you'll see *(visual language)* that we have a practical and easy way to implement a growth solution for you *(lead, this is the suggestion I want the client to take onboard as being true, and it's a hook).*

"As you know from the meetings leading up to today *(pace, we have had meetings),* we have taken time to really understand the challenges you're currently facing *(pace, we have asked the client questions about their challenges).* Almost more importantly, this understanding is also based upon where you want to be in three years from now *(pace, it's what they want and know)* and it's this that we want to focus on today *(pace);* how we can best help you achieve these results. Our aim is to simply show you how you can achieve the growth you want *(lead, visual language).*

Growth slide

As you can see *(visual language)* from this slide, we believe we can meet your future growth targets by focusing on two main areas *(pace, it's in the slide).* They are, targeting your current customers and helping you to attract new customers *(pace, again it's in the slide)*. By improving your ability to attract and retain a higher share of your customers *(pace, they already know this)*, we believe you could make significant increases in the overall growth of your business *(pace, they already know this)*. In fact, we estimate that within a two-year period, you could see your sales grow by over 20% *(lead, starting to talk about our solution and hook)*. But, that's not all. This forecasted growth is only part of the story, because we'll also explain *(auditory language)* how we can reduce the unit cost of acquiring new customers for you *(lead, starting to talk about the solution and hook)*.

Before we get into the details of how this can be achieved *(hook)*, I would like to take this opportunity to introduce John. John has worked for us for over four years, during which time he has won two industry awards *(covert credentials, attaching values or capitalise on their supporting beliefs)* and has been an integral part of helping us to a top ten ranking *(covert credentials, attaching values or capitalise on their supporting beliefs)*. John..."

"Thank you. As we are all aware, the world we live in has changed considerably over the last few years *(pace, it has and emotional language)* and sometimes it seems to be happening more rapidly than we can reasonably keep up with *(pace, true and emotional language)*. Whilst we are in the throes of change *(emotional language)* it can be easy to lose sight *(visual language)* of the long-term objectives *(pace, yes we can)*. So today, as Marcus has said *(pace, auditory language)*, we want to focus *(visual language)* on where you want to get to as a brand, not what might stop us from getting there *(lead, and pre-frame)*. So Let's start by..."

As you can see, it's very easy to start to put these ideas together and on the face of it, using Pacing and Leading statements, opening hooks, visual, auditory and emotional language and pre-framing just sounds like normal conversation, but it is so much more than that. This is what will give you the power to really manage and influence the emotional state of your clients during your pitch. Have a look at this opening again and, as you read through it, ask yourself what emotions you think your clients might be feeling if they were to listen to it? Then have a look at this paragraph and notice all of the Pacing and Leading I have done. To get good at these techniques it's going to take awareness and practice.

Now we have looked at your introduction, let's move on to the middle section of your pitch.

Putting it All Together:
The Middle of Your Pitch

By the time you get to the middle section of your pitch, your clients should be emotionally engaged in your content. In your introduction, you have outlined a solution for them. Also, you've opened hooks for things you want people to listen out for. You should have given them lots of Why with not much detail, so they will be looking for what those percentages actually mean in real terms. You have elicited values from as many key players as possible (advanced questions) and are now ready to start using them and you should have Paced and Led your clients, so they are with you logically as well.

There are so many ways you could construct the middle of you pitch, I'm going to outline things you need to think about, rather than offer a prescriptive formula. Remember that you have to add information in a way that allows your clients to accept your solution, Pacing and Leading. Remember to use the *4MAT System* for each individual section.

There are a number of key things about which to think.

Firstly, as you design your pitch, try to have an individual section for the key decision makers. I know this isn't always feasible, but if they know you have something just for them it will make them feel special. The other reason why you might want to do this is because it gives you somewhere to attach their values statement. When you use the *4MAT System* to structure the content for each individual, it means that the benefits/results slide comes at the end of that section (**What if**) and that's where you want to attach the values statement. By the time they get to the benefit slide, they will have had all the logical reasons for buying your solution. You make it personal to the individuals by attaching their value statement to it. This satisfies both company and personal motivations.

The second thing you need to do in the middle part of your presentation is neutralise any limiting beliefs held by your clients. In the section on beliefs we looked at a number of ways you could do this and I'm going to give my preferred way here. I like to use pre-frames in the introduction or even in your pre-pitch meetings, because they are incredibly powerful. Then when I get to the section where the client's limiting belief will be triggered, I'm going to suggest you give detail. Lots of it. People get worried by uncertainty. They like to know what's going to happen. Giving detail shows that their future is mapped out, that you have done it before, and that you have catered for all eventualities. My objective, by this stage, is to help my clients to feel comfortable, so that they are no longer worried about their concerns. Finally, after the detail I use a testimonial. Using a testimonial is just the icing on the cake. If there are any remaining concerns, hearing how you helped a client who shared the same concerns get what they wanted and how they were able to produce great results with you, is enough to neutralise most limiting beliefs.

You also need to capitalise on the supporting beliefs your client holds about you. During the middle section, give examples of how you could deliver on these beliefs. You don't need to overplay this, but you do need to do it. Using a testimonial is a useful way to achieve this. If your client's supporting belief is that you could reduce costs for them, show a testimonial from a client you're currently working with and have them mention reduced costs as one of the benefits. In addition, I have already mentioned linking supporting beliefs as you introduce a colleague.

Finally, in your middle section, you need to resolve the emotional hooks you have opened. In the introduction above, I said that we can reduce the unit cost of acquiring new customers, and at some point in your presentation you have to talk about how you will achieve this. I'm going to refer to this as closing the hook. Because I come from a film background, I like to reference movies to describe how opening and closing hooks works.

If you think about a film, it's made up of lots of two to three minute scenes that weave in and out of the main plot. You have an overall plot or theme; in your case it might be helping your client grow their customer base, or reducing their costs, etc. You also have your sub-plots. These are the individual sections of your bridge that support your main theme. In the movies, these sub-plots open and close all the time during the film. Have you noticed that movies start a sub-plot and just when it's getting interesting they move on to something else. Then they come back to the sub-plot later and show you a little more of it. This is opening and closing the hooks. In your pitch you can't do exactly the same, but when you create an emotional hook, by talking about something that's coming up, you can open and close them in the same way. If you have sections during your pitch where someone hasn't been engaged with for a while, open a hook for them. Be upfront and say that you will be getting to them shortly or that we are going to look at reducing costs after this next section. Similarly, you can close a hook during a long, less engaging section of your pitch. The movies do this brilliantly, they close hooks in the second act, to keep the plot moving forward and to hold your attention. More about this in the section on Metaphors, in Part Three. Oops, there's another hook!

Putting it All Together: The End of Your Pitch

I don't know if you have ever noticed this, but in some restaurants they have a great starter and a great pudding and the bit in the middle can be, well, the bit in the middle. Restaurants know that you will remember the last thing you eat.

The pudding is the bit that just rounds off the meal. The days of huge wedges of spotted dick and dollops of lumpy, cold custard are over (thank God). Restaurants want you to leave feeling happy and know that you've had an enjoyable experience.

By the end of your presentation, you want to give your clients a lift, not weigh them down with dollops of lumpy information. Like a great restaurant, you're just rounding off the meal, so your clients feel great, committed and leave happy. By this stage, your clients should believe that they can have what they most want. If they don't, they probably never will and doling out wedges and dollops here and there, isn't going to help.

Keep it light, even entertaining, remember you always have questions. Summarise, give the highlights and keep it short, the sell is over. What are the two or three key things you want clients to take away from your pitch? The end is about how you want to be remembered. If you want to be remembered as someone who laboured on trying to sell, do that, but I'm not sure how much it will help you. All you'll do is bore the client, they will disengage and that's what they will remember (spotted dick and cold custard).

Think about how you're going to end your pitch, about how you're going to invite questions and, possibly, what questions you might like to be asked.

Summary

- It's easy to hide powerful language techniques in your introduction. These language techniques will help you manage your client's emotional states.

- Use the *4MAT* System for each section of your pitch.

- Having individual sections for the key decision makers will help them to feel special. It also means you have somewhere to attach their values statement.

- You should have started to neutralise your clients limiting beliefs already, so in the middle section try giving detailed information and using a testimonial.

- Capitalise on their supporting beliefs.

- During the middle section of your pitch, you will start to close the emotional hooks you've opened.

- By the end of your pitch, the sell is over.

- Keep it short. It's how you want your client to remember you.

Exercises

- Incorporate a number of techniques that would be useful in your pitch, like Pacing and Leading, language types, emotional hooks and practise them.

- Work out a plan for neutralising your client's biggest limiting beliefs.

- Execute it.

- Practice makes perfect. Rehearse your content. Get good at using the language techniques we have talked about.

- Rehearse how you're going to pass rapport from presenter to presenter and also how you're going to introduce each other.

- Practise what you are going to say in your section of the pitch, and practise your pitch as a group as well. This way everyone gets to see who's opening and closing what hooks etc.

As we come to the end of Part Two, please rate how much more persuasive you believe you could be in your next pitch as a result of the information you now have. Please write your percentage improvement score below.

PART THREE

ADVANCED PITCH
STRATEGIES

1.
LANGUAGE

How to use language more persuasively in your pitch

THE BIG DAY HAS ARRIVED. It's pitch time.

You have a great solution, you have a brilliant presentation, now it's time to write what you're going to say.

In this section, we're going to look at three ways you can use your language to have the greatest emotional impact on your clients.

Firstly, there is something known as internal representations. These are the pictures you make when people communicate with you. For you to understand what they're saying, you have to make an internal representation of what they're talking about. For example, the dog was in the yard. For you to make sense of this sentence you have to make some kind of internal representation of the dog and the yard. You're not consciously aware of this process, but it goes on all the time. So, to test this, what colour is your dog? Really think about it.

Whatever colour you thought of, you're right. It's your dog. Now, what is the dog doing?

By answering these questions, you are becoming aware of the internal representations you are making. So, how is this useful in a pitch? When you pitch, you will be forcing internal representations onto your clients. As you communicate with them in all of your pre-pitch meetings, documents, and the pitch itself, you want to make sure you are forcing positive internal representations into their minds. You can literally control the pictures your clients make in their minds when you talk to them.

I'm going to suggest that you keep your language as positive as possible during your interaction with your client. This way you will be forcing positive internal representations into their minds. Here's an example: *you're wrong*, versus, *you're not always right*. In essence they mean the same thing but what internal pictures do you create with *you're wrong*? Think about it for a second. For me, when I think of *you're wrong*, I think of being told off by a Dickensian style teacher, a dark murky image that makes me feel inadequate and insecure. But the picture I make with *you're not always right*, is of me smiling, it's a bright sunny picture, it makes me feel good. It's the same message, but it creates two very different internal pictures for me. Positive language really does have a positive effect on your clients. So in your pitch you need to avoid negative language; instead, try to flip what you need to say as a negative, into a positive. Instead of saying "We're defending a pitch", why not say "We have an opportunity to keep the client"? Instead of saying, "We've made mistakes", why not say "We've done our best"?

Changing your language changes the pictures your clients make, and this changes their experience of what's happening. This will have a direct bearing on their emotional state. As I said above, *you're not always right* makes me feel good. My positive emotional experience of a helpful criticism keeps me happy. This entire book is about emotions. If I make you feel good, special or important, then you will be much more inclined to want to work with me. Your emails, your documents, the headings on your slides, the language you use during the pitch and the language you use to answer your client's questions, all force internal images into your client's mind. The more positive you can make them, the better you make your clients feel.

The second way of controlling your client's emotions is by using Emotional Impact Words. Based upon the work of Igor Ledochowski[1], Emotional Impact Words are words that tap into the client's own deep emotions. Language is full of emotion, and Emotional Impact Words are words that fire off positive or negative emotions within us. Imagine that right now I said to you the name of someone you really loved, like your partner or one of your children. Imagine you could hear me saying their name. Did you smile? Did it make you feel good? It should have. Words have amazing power. Think about words like, love, hope, happiness and freedom. They fire off positive emotions for you. Now think about, hate, war and murder. These words fire off negative emotions. Somewhere in between these two extremes of language are words we use all the time in business. Obviously, the less extreme the word, the finer the emotional distinction becomes.

What words are you using in your documents or your pitch right now that you could change to have a greater emotional impact? Instead of *produce results*, why not use *produce greater success*? What words have positive associations with your client? Are they caring and kind? Or are they driven, successful, fast tracked, motivated, go-getters? Once you realise what Emotional Impact Words resonate with your individual clients, you can feed these words back to them during the pitch, firing off deep positive emotions within them.

Create some Emotional Impact Words or phrases that would generically work with each individual. Have words that fire off positive emotions for: Procurement, the CEO, the Marketing Director, the Sales Director. Try them out during the pre-pitch meetings and calibrate their response. If they react favourably to these Emotional Impact Words, you know they would be good to use in the pitch. Similarly, if you're in the pre-pitch meeting and the client says something that fires them up in a positive way, they have just used their own Emotional Impact Word, so make a note of that word to use in the pitch where appropriate.

Finally, you need to keep your audience attentive during the pitch. With some pitches being several hours long and over 100 slides, clients are bound to drift off. So you really need to think about ways you can help your clients remain focused. There are a number of words you can use to re-focus your clients onto your content, such as *look, now, focus, OK.* These are words that snap your client's focus back to your pitch. *Let's take a moment to look at this... Now, I want to show you... Let's focus on... OK, in this next slide...*

The other great thing about using words that re-focus attention is you can use them to emphasise a point you want to make. Say the re-focus word, then make the point. By snapping attention back to you and your content at the right moment, and then making your important point, you are making sure that the client is focused and fully engaged with you before you deliver the information. Now, is that a useful thing to know?

Summary
- When you communicate with your clients (written or verbally) you are forcing images into their mind.
- Making your language more positive creates more positive internal representations. Which in turn helps to manage their emotional state.

- Similarly, Emotional Impact Words are words that manage your client's emotional state.
- It will help you to know what kinds of words individual clients respond well to, and words to which they don't respond well.
- Re-focus words allow you to re-engage your client's attention during your pitch.

Exercises

- Think about what internal representations you are forcing on your clients during your pitch. Are they the ones you want to be forcing?
- In your pitch, you want to excite your clients about their future and build commitment. Think about the words and therefore internal representations you would need to use to achieve this.
- Make a list of generic Emotional Impact Words to try with different individual clients in your pre-pitch meetings.
- Start to use words that re-focus attention during your pitch.

2.
THE POWER OF
SOCIAL PROOF

How to use testimonials more
persuasively in your pitch

I HAVE MENTIONED TESTIMONIALS ON a number of occasions during this book but I haven't really explained how to use them in detail. A testimonial is the social proof that says you can produce the results you're promising. The object of a testimonial is to remove the barriers to winning the pitch.

To use testimonials effectively in your pitch, ask yourself the reasons this client might have for not buying from you. Make a list. If you have asked the right questions (see limiting beliefs in Advanced Questions), you should know these answers. Then all you do is ask yourself how many clients you are currently working with who had similar challenges when they first joined you?

Using a testimonial that mirrors your clients concerns will create the greatest emotional impact, because it resonates more deeply with their point of view, their challenges and concerns. You want to demonstrate that you understand your client, that they can trust you and believe that you can help them.

This is what this type of mirroring testimonial does. Don't just have any old testimonial, because it invokes a "So what?" response from your client. Neither do you just want testimonials that say how great you are because again, *"So what?"*

To increase the power of your mirroring testimonial, present a before and after scenario. You want the client you're currently working with to talk about how you moved them from A to B and what kind of difference it made to their business. The differences you made to their business are their benefit statements about you.

As I have mentioned before, testimonials are a covert way of getting your benefits across. So what benefits does your client want? More money, more customers, cheaper deals? Whatever it is, this is the benefit your current client needs to get across in their testimonial. So, the structure of your testimonial is:

1. Current client talks about their problem/concern/challenge.
2. They talk about how your company helped them by suggesting ABC, which they applied by doing XYZ. The testimonial needs to outline your recommendations and how they were applied (details in a testimonial are good for neutralising a limiting belief). This then becomes an opportunity for your client to see the different ways they could

implement your advice and ideas. It's third party learning.

3. Now they no longer have this problem/ concern/ challenge. They have produced these results/benefits (increased profitability, more customers, etc).

If you want to use more than one testimonial in your pitch, great, go for it. As long as your testimonials address the client's concerns, you can tag on a different benefit, just make sure it's a benefit your client wants.

So, what kind of testimonials work best? In a word: video. You can't fudge a video testimonial. You can see the person, you can hear their voice, you can look into their eyes as they speak. Always have their name and job description and company name on the testimonial. You don't want the client to think: "Yeah, ok, but I don't buy that." Most video testimonials have a powerful impact on their audience. Written testimonials are less powerful because, let's face it, anyone could have written them. So wherever possible, use video. As well as being more powerful, they are a great way to break up your pitch, to let someone else do the talking for a change.

Which brings me on to who do you get to do your testimonial? Of course there are the clients you're currently working with and I'm sure many of them would be happy to help you. Or how about someone your client wants to be like? If they are a small company who wants to grow into a big company, use a testimonial from a client whose company you helped to grow. As with everything, put your client at the heart of your thinking. Think about who they would feel most reassured by. If they could ask any of your current clients, who would they ask?

As a note – and it's really my preference – don't just get one client to do all your different testimonials. I think it looks like you haven't really bothered to make an effort. But that's just me.

There is another way you could use a testimonial. If you have a strategy or proposal that you think your clients might find challenging, a testimonial from an authority figure that supports your proposal can do wonders for your case. Obviously you want someone your client has heard of, trusts and respects. In the same way that social proof is a powerful influencer, so is the use of an authority figure.

Finally, if you make credentials presentations and subtlety is not appropriate, adopting the ideas outlined above will make your presentation more relevant and engaging for the client.

Summary

- Testimonials are a good way to remove any final barriers your clients might have.

- When finding a client to use in your testimonial, look for someone who mirrors your client's situation closely.

- Use a before and after scenario, with a benefit at the end.

- Video testimonials are more convincing.

- Who do you use in your testimonial? Find someone your client wants to be like, or use an expert to support your advice.

Exercises

- If you use a testimonial, be very clear on the information you expect your current client to deliver. Don't waste time by letting them talk about things that aren't relevant or useful. Manage the process. If a testimonial has lots of edits in it, it undermines its credibility.

3.
ADVANCED
METAPHOR DESIGN

How to be more Emotionally
Persuasive with metaphors

WHAT IS A METAPHOR AND how can it make you more persuasive in your pitch?

I'm going to explain a metaphor as a story that has many levels of communication. You have the story itself (the words you use), you have the meaning of the story (the underlying message), you also have all the covert strategies and language patterns that can be contained within that story. The power of the metaphor is that your messages aren't communicated in a direct way. Therefore they contain the power to change minds or sell without conscious resistance from your client.

In this chapter, we'll look at why you should use metaphors and how you can create metaphors with their own hidden meanings.

There are many types of metaphor. We are going to look at metaphors contained within stories and pictures.

I'm going to start with stories, because these are the most common type of metaphor. Most people hear lots of different stories every day. Stories about how a colleague got to work, the work they are doing, their clients, their boss, their partner, their night out and about the day they've had. We all hear lots of stories all day long and because we are used to telling and hearing stories from each other, we assume they are just that, a story – but not all of them are.

In the section on Pacing and Leading, I mentioned something known as the critical factor. The critical factor is your conscious reasoning. It's the little voice in your head that says: "Hang on a minute, I'm not sure about this." The critical factor is the gatekeeper to your unconscious mind. Once you bypass the critical factor, you're bypassing the filter that judges the information you're receiving. When information enters into the unconscious mind it is more readily accepted as being true. Because we are used to hearing stories from different sources all day, our critical factor goes offline and doesn't judge the information it's hearing because it's just another story.

This technique has been used as a therapeutic tool or to promote behavioural change for thousands of years. We tell stories that help us to learn from other people's experiences, and we tell stories of how someone else dealt with a similar problem that a friend of ours is now facing. We tell stories to motivate people and we tell stories to relax people. Stories really are as old as the hills. Think about how religion uses stories. Most people could recite a story from their own religion. Many of these stories convey a message. We might not get the story factually correct, but we would get the essence of it and more than likely the meaning of the message it contained. And that's the power of metaphors. Memorable messages.

In your pitch, there are a number of ways you might want to use a metaphor. I'm going to talk about three types of metaphor, why they are different and how you can construct and use them. The first type is an Emotional Metaphor, which is designed to elicit specific emotional states in your clients. The second type is a Meaning Metaphor, designed to convey hidden meaning. The third type is known as an Isomorphic Metaphor, which is designed to resolve a problem or challenge that your client is facing. How you decide which metaphors to use will be determined by your clients and what messages you think they need to hear, or what emotional states you want to elicit from them.

For your metaphors to have real power, the subject matter you choose to contain your message or emotion, the wrapper, has to be interesting and relevant to your client. There are two ways to design your metaphor to make it interesting. Firstly, you can tell a story about something you know a client is interested in. Sport is an obvious choice, if they support a team or an individual sports personality that gives you a whole area around which to create metaphors. However, because it's specific to one individual, it might have a limited appeal in your pitch. Business is another example, and this is likely to have a wider appeal. My second type of metaphor is based on universal themes. These are themes that everyone can understand and relate to. There are lots of universal themes like kindness, love, happiness, humour, struggle, collaboration, common goals, freedom, achievement. There are also themes like childhood, the first day in a new job, family holidays, Christmas, school, relationships, moving into a new home. Because most people have experienced these things, it means that they can relate to your story and they can engage with it.

If your clients don't engage with your metaphor, then you will find it hard to elicit emotional states from them, or to get your hidden message or solution across. So finding the right story as a wrapper for your message or emotion is something you need to think about.

Before we look at these three types of metaphor in detail, let's look at how you can use them. You can start your metaphor before the pitch or you can start it during the pitch. You can start a metaphor and not finish it; this is known as an open loop metaphor. You can start a metaphor in the pre-pitch meetings and end it in the pitch; this is known as closing the loop. You can use a number of metaphors or just one. You can use a metaphor that directly mirrors something about your client or one that doesn't. You can use a metaphor that is packed with strategies and things you want your clients to do. Now you know what you can do with a metaphor, let's look at how you can design your own.

Type 1. Metaphors that elicit emotions

Let's start by looking at designing metaphors to elicit specific emotional states in your clients. As I have been saying all the way through, managing emotions in your pitch is critical. When you are in a bad mood you treat people differently to when you are in a good mood. The same is true for your clients sitting in your pitch. If they are in a bad mood it changes the way they engage with you, the way they listen to you, and what they remember from your pitch.

That's why you need to manage their emotional state. We've already looked at useful emotional states in your pitch (the introduction to Part Two) and at a number of ways you can elicit them. Emotional metaphors are just another way to elicit these useful emotional states.

Here's how you design and use a metaphor to elicit an emotional state in your client.

Start with the emotional state you want to elicit. It has to be positive and, if you are using emotional metaphors in your pitch, it's going to help you if you elicit a state that is useful for learning (curiosity, interest, excitement). Once you have chosen your emotional state, think of a couple of times in your life when you felt that emotion strongly, where this was the overriding emotion of that event. Make a list of those times and what you were you doing. If you can't think of an event from your life, how about from someone close to you, where this emotion was present for them? Now, which one of these stories would your client find most interesting? Which one would resonate best with them? Pick that story. Write down as much detail as you can remember about it. This is important, because the more detail you can recall the more your metaphor will come to life. As you relive the story, you will relive that emotion, and all your non-verbal communication will reflect this. Make notes on paper, don't just think about it in your head; writing things down helps.

Here's an example of a story I sometimes tell to get people into a state of curiosity.

"Earlier this year I bought a brilliant mentalist's routine on the internet. It was one of these routines which allows you to really read someone's mind. That's right, it tells you step by step how to actually read someone's mind, and it's not just guessing, it's naming someone's boyfriend when you have never met them before, or their mother's maiden name or pet, or whatever you liked. It's a fabulous routine but, as a gift, I was sent an even more brilliant card trick, which you can also dress up as mentalist routine. I love card tricks and this is one of the best tricks I have ever seen. I used to drive my friends mad with my old card tricks, so as soon as I saw this one, I knew I had something really special. Everything was online, so I watched the card trick through and my chin hit the floor. It was amazing. Here's a quick description. The punter takes nine cards from anywhere in the deck and gives them to the mentalist. The mentalist takes the cards and, without looking at them, puts them face down on the table. The mentalist then writes something on a piece of paper and puts the paper to one side. One by one, the nine cards are chosen at random by both the punter and the mentalist until they are left with just one card. The mentalist retrieves his piece of paper and gives it to the punter who reads it aloud. The paper has the details of a card written on it. The punter flips over the last card to reveal that it's the same as the card written on the paper. I watched it again and again, but I still couldn't figure it out. I was bursting to know how to do this amazing card trick. Eventually, I couldn't wait any longer so I pressed play to reveal how the trick is done, and oh my..."

Now, if you're someone who's interested in card tricks or mentalism, then I guess you might want to know how this brilliant, but simple, trick is done. If you are interested, then I've made you curious. I have led you into the emotional state of curiosity by writing about the trick. In fact, I might have slightly overdone things, because some of you might be so curious that you are annoyed because I haven't revealed how the trick is done. This is opening the emotional loop. If you don't like mentalism or card tricks, then the wrapper I've used has no impact on you and you won't be in a state of curiosity.

When I want to use this type of emotional metaphor, I recall the event clearly in my mind. The more I recall it, the more I'm reliving it. The more I relive it, the more I get into that emotional state. This applies to any emotional state you want to get into. Relive a memory and you will start to go into the emotional state that was present during the memory. When I think about the time I first saw this trick my tonality changes to become curious and when I tell you about this trick, my tonal shift draws you even more into my world, into my metaphor. My unconscious non-verbal cues change; imagine my expression as I watched the trick again and again to see if I could tell how it was done, the concentration and amazement on my face. Everything about me reflects my curiosity as I relive and tell this metaphor. If I get into a state of curiosity, then I will start to create that state in other people. The key to doing this is to make sure that your metaphor only contains one emotional state. If you have two emotional states competing against each other, especially if one is positive and one is negative, then as you relive this story, you will be putting yourself through both states and there probably won't be a clear enough distinction between them for you or your client. This is a common mistake.

Here's the rule: one metaphor, one emotional state. Don't confuse your client by trying to elicit more than one state per story. Also, remember that emotional states take time to well up. If you go for more than one emotional state, then there's a good chance that you will rush one state at the expense of the other and you might well end up with nothing at all or a state you didn't want – confusion. Allow time to tell the story. To make the state stronger for your client, tell the story using all the different language types. In my metaphor I used different language types and lots of descriptive words to describe the trick, which helped to bring it to life for you. When we tell stories to each other, we give descriptions and we paint vivid pictures in the minds of the listener. Telling a metaphor is no different.

Another key to eliciting an emotional state is to talk around the emotion. Don't just say: "I got curious." Tell them about it. How did you get curious? What was it like for you when you did get curious? I also used the set-up to engage your curiosity. Firstly, I moved straight past the mind-reading routine, which implies that somehow the trick I'm going to tell you about must be more impressive than that.

Let's be honest, mind-reading is about as impressive as it gets! So your expectation about what

I'm going to tell you is already heightened. Secondly, I told you how I drive my friends mad with my old card tricks and this one is better. The sub-text of what I have just said is that this trick must be great, therefore you will want to know about it. Again, I'm setting up your expectation, so that by the time I tell you about the trick you're already primed and wanting to know about it. These set-up techniques really help to build in more curiosity. When you are creating your metaphor, think about all the little embellishments and set-ups you could use, to make the experience even more powerful and engaging for your client. Describe the experience; the more real it is for you, the more real it becomes for them. Relive the experience and they will live it too.

So, you have your story, you've added everything you need to add to make it as real as possible, engaging to listen to and you can elicit the emotional state you want. Now, what do you do with it? How do you use it?

Firstly, you can tell your emotional metaphor as an open loop. This means, right at the moment where your metaphor has reached its emotional peak, about 80-90% into the story, you stop the story abruptly. Change the subject and move on to delivering your content. When you stop a metaphor at its emotional peak, you are really engaging your clients emotionally. If I told you how to do the trick, you wouldn't be curious any more. As soon as your clients reach this heightened emotional state, this is the moment for you to start delivering your content. If you get them into a state of curiosity or excitement about what they are going to learn, they will take these heightened emotional states into your content and will engage with the information in a more powerful way. Look at what I did in my metaphor. By not telling you how the trick is done, I opened a loop. As soon as it's open, what did I do? I started to deliver my content. At some point after you have delivered your content, it's a good idea to close the loop, by concluding the story. Closing the loop bookends your content.

There's another advantage to stopping your metaphor before its natural conclusion. When you do this, your client's unconscious mind will be listening out for the conclusion. Everything that you deliver between opening and closing the loop will have the attention of their unconscious mind. So where do you open and close loops? You can open a loop anywhere, from your pre-pitch meetings when you are just chatting, or in the pitch itself. I would recommend that you open a loop before you start delivering content, for the reasons mentioned above. You can close a loop during the pitch, at the end of your pitch or after it has finished.

You might be thinking to yourself, I could never do this, it just wouldn't work in a pitch. OK, I understand that, because I haven't really explained how you can open and close loops in a pitch yet. So let me tell you a story I heard about someone who, just before a pitch started, told a story about something his kids had done that morning. This story acted as an icebreaker, it was funny and charming. It put the client at ease, it engaged them, it disarmed them and more importantly, it put them into a positive emotional state. Now, suppose that this funny, charming story is actually very relevant to a point that's going to be made later on in the pitch. Now you have something really powerful. All you do to create this link is refer back to the charming story from earlier. When you do this you will be firing off those emotions in your clients again. This is particularly useful if you have come to a part of your pitch where you want your clients fully engaged and in a specific emotional state. When you link back to the story, you are closing the loop you have opened. Let's say, in your funny charming story about your kids, your kids are haggling over the cost of something. To make the link in your pitch, you just talk about how you will haggle (in the same way your kids did) over costs with your suppliers. It's going to help you if you go back to standing or sitting in the same spot from where you delivered the first part of your metaphor. If you can, it will also help if you can use the same tonality.

So, instead of just telling a story, why not give it some emotion, give it a purpose and why not link it, if you can, to something in your pitch? Getting clients into a positive emotional state is easy to do. You can use your metaphor in the pitch room, in reception, in the lift on the way up to your offices, or weeks before in a pre-pitch meeting. It doesn't matter where. Get creative, try things out, test and measure. Did your metaphor produce the results you were expecting? Did your metaphor lighten their mood and get them in the emotional state you wanted? If not, why not? What could you do differently next time? If you think about it, talking about a client you've helped is a metaphor as well; how might that make them feel? Reassured, confident in your ability? Maybe that's how you get them excited about what you could do for them. The list is endless. Just start thinking about the emotional states you want your clients to experience and then think of stories from your life that they might want to hear about. Always start with the emotional state you think will benefit their experience of your pitch. If you don't want to try this idea out in a pitch, try it out with a client you're working with in a meeting. See how you get on. Pitches and meetings shouldn't be deathly boring. Have some fun, you never know – your clients might enjoy it too.

The card trick really is brilliant, and for those of you who need to know how it's done, and to close the loop for everyone else, after I have delivered the content, here's the link:

www.mentalismnow.com/marcuscorah.html

That's how you put emotions into metaphors, but how about putting in a message? How do you build up layers of communication, so ideas slide into your client's mind, without resistance?

Type 2. Metaphors that convey hidden messages and benefits

Have you ever wanted to give a client a piece of advice, but didn't because you knew they would reject it out of hand? By layering messages into a metaphor, you can convey the essence of what you want to say without saying it directly. This dramatically increases the chances of your message being acted upon. Moreover, if you add a benefit into this message, you increase the chances that the message will be acted upon even more.

To design a metaphor with a message you need to start with the end in mind. What message do you want to convey and how does this message benefit your client? There's a useful formula to help structure these types of metaphors. The formula is: **Incident, Point, Benefit.**

Think of an incident from your life, that has a point and a benefit.

The **Incident** is the event that happened to you – the wrapper for your story. It might be when you were walking down a road, or swimming in the sea, or eating lunch, it doesn't matter. All we need is some context to wrap around what you were doing and what happened.

The **Point** is your hidden message. So what message do you want to convey in your metaphor?

The **Benefit** is the benefit of your hidden message to your client. If you have a benefit that's of interest to your client, it provides the motivation they need to act on your hidden message.

When you're creating your **Incident**, **Point**, **Benefit** metaphor, you can start with the incident or the benefit. If you start with an incident, then you need to create a benefit. Or, you can start with the benefit and then work backwards to an incident. I'm going to suggest that you start with a benefit and work backwards. I think if you're going to tell a story, and you might only tell one, it should have a strong clear benefit and if possible be tailored to your client's needs or wants. In my opinion, working this way around is the best way to get your message across.

Here is how you create a metaphor, working back from the benefit. Let's say your client wants more new customers. They have a concern about your approach because it means that they will have to try something they haven't tried before and this worries them. Just coming out and saying you have to do it this way or else could make them feel uncomfortable, which means there's a good chance they would reject the idea.

The **point** of the metaphor is to get your client to consider trying something new, this is the hidden message you want to convey. The **benefit** to the client is more new customers and therefore financial reward.

Here's the metaphor:

"I was walking to pick my daughter up from school the other day and decided I would go a different way. I get bored of going the same way all the time and besides, it was a beautiful, bright sunny afternoon, so I thought, why not walk on the sunny side of the street? As I walked along this new route, I got stuck behind a couple of mothers chatting and cooing over their babies in their prams. They moved slowly because they were so engaged in their own conversation. I was about to walk past them when I noticed a five pound note on the ground right in front of me. I was amazed they hadn't seen it, but I guess they were just too engaged in their conversation. I smiled to myself, picked up the money and took my daughter for a treat after school. I hadn't had a chance to do this for a while, because of work, so we got an opportunity to bond."

In my story, the wrapper, the **incident**, is picking up my daughter from school. The **point** or hidden message I want to convey is that I want them to take a different route. Now, on its own, taking a different route has no incentive for the client, that's why I have to attach a benefit to the action I want them to take. The **benefit** in my metaphor is finding the money and bonding with someone I care about. Logically, if the client gets more customers that means they will be making more money, hence using money as part of the benefit. This money resulted in the opportunity to bond with my daughter, something most clients are looking to do with their customers. There are a couple of other points to consider in this metaphor. Firstly, notice how I used different language types when I was giving reasons for going a different way. *It was a beautiful, bright sunny afternoon, so I thought why not try a different route?* By using three different language types like this, I'm engaging the clients more emotionally to the idea. This means they are more likely to remember this important part of the message. Secondly, if you want to get sneaky, the mothers could represent your competitors, not aware of what is going on or not noticing opportunities. You could use a metaphor to describe your competitors, are they big and lumbering, or lean? Do they have a big family or are they a small outfit?

You could tailor this story to meet pretty much any benefit your clients wanted to achieve. If you think about it, you could take this idea and create literally hundreds of metaphors around taking a different route, which allows you to tailor the benefit to your different clients and the message they need to hear.

It probably takes thirty seconds to tell a metaphor like this. If you wanted to, you could link this metaphor to your content during your pitch. At some point you'll probably be talking about making your clients more money and there's the link. All you need to do to reference the metaphor by saying something like: "This is the direction we suggest you take because it will produce a much greater ROI for you as well as strengthen your customer bond." You've just linked your metaphor, which is about trying something new, to your pitch.

Type 3. Metaphors that resolve a problem

Imagine being able to tell a story to a client, that covertly gives your clients a solution to a challenge they are facing. There's a metaphor known as an isomorphic metaphor, which does just that.

An isomorphic metaphor works because it reflects the real situation that your client is experiencing. By making a comparison between your metaphor and their real life challenge, you can offer them a solution contained within your metaphor.

Because isomorphic metaphors need to reflect real life challenges, it's not always the case that you will have your own life experience to draw upon. This means you can reference other people's experiences or just make up a story that reflects your client's circumstances closely. There are three things to consider when constructing an isomorphic metaphor: the current situation or challenge for your client, the number of people involved and your solution to their challenge.

Let me give you an example of how I used an isomorphic metaphor. This metaphor isn't to do with a pitch, so please bear with me.

A couple of years ago, Charlotte (not her real name) who was five, got stuck in a lift. Her father, grandmother and grandfather were there at the time and tried to help her. After about five minutes Charlotte managed to get the lift working again, but as you might imagine, it was a scary experience for a young girl. To help her, I came up with this isomorphic metaphor.

"One day, a beautiful princess called Charlotte (Charlotte loved princesses and her real name started with C) was travelling to meet the handsome prince (her father) whom she was planning to marry, but on her journey she had to travel through a big, dark forest (the lift). As Princess Charlotte went further into the forest she noticed that the trees were starting to block out more and more sunlight (she found the lift scary because it only had one light). Princess Charlotte started to get frightened as she travelled further into the forest. Before long, Princess Charlotte and her horse came across a beautiful lake surrounded by flowers and all kinds of pretty things. So she stopped there to let her horse drink from the lake's cool waters. As the horse drank, Princess Charlotte sat and waited. Suddenly there was a strange sound nearby which caused the horse to bolt, leaving the princess all alone.

At first she was frightened because of the sounds coming from the forest. The princess could hear voices but couldn't see anyone (this is what happened because her father, grandmother and grandfather were shouting to her to make sure she was OK). Then she started to see little fairies coming to see who she was, and what she was doing in the forest all alone. The fairies took care of Princess Charlotte, they played games with her, stroked her hair and made sure she had plenty to eat and drink so that the princess wouldn't be scared anymore. In fact, she enjoyed playing with the forest fairies so much that she didn't hear the prince come riding up. The princess' horse had run all the way through the forest and had been caught by a kind farmer who had raised the alarm. On hearing the news, the prince had ridden into the forest to look for his true love. He vowed then never to leave her side and they were married by the king and queen the very next day (to help Charlotte over the event, everyone made her a special tea). The wedding ceremony was the most beautiful ceremony anyone had ever seen. All the princess' favourite friends came and the palace was filled with joy and laughter all day and they all lived happily ever after."

In the story above, I mirrored the real life events experienced by Charlotte very closely. I offered a solution to the event by talking about the forest in a positive way and how it wasn't the scary place that she first thought it was because the fairies made her feel welcome. Then I talked about the prince coming to rescue her and ultimately how they lived happily ever after.

An isomorphic metaphor is much more effective if you create a story about something your audience likes and cares about. With Charlotte, I took the story one step away from the reality of the original situation (the lift), for two reasons. Firstly, you don't want to trigger off the original negative emotional state associated with the lift, because it will make it much harder to work towards a positive change in their attitude. Secondly, if I talk about the lift there is no room to elaborate the story or have any other outcomes which produce a positive solution. Consciously, Charlotte isn't aware of the story being related to what happened in the lift, the metaphor relies on her unconscious mind making a connection between the event and the story and then re-interpreting the event in a positive light.

As you might have realised, isomorphic metaphors are a great way to break up a limiting belief because you are able to offer a better solution or belief to the client, than that which they are currently holding. To use an isomorphic metaphor in a pitch, you have to first understand your client's predicament or concern, then find a story that's a good vehicle to carry a solution. In the section on beliefs, I told an isomorphic metaphor, about getting stuck in Europe. If you go back and re-read it with the knowledge you now have, you'll find you can draw a completely different meaning from it. You'll find it in Part One, in the *beliefs and pitching* section.

Here's another way you can use isomorphic metaphors. In training sessions, I use them as a way of pre-teaching a solution to some of the content of the session. Over the years I have found that as good as training sessions are, within a matter of weeks, some delegates slip back into their old habits. One of the ways I get round this is to help delegates to come up with their own solutions; this way they own the ideas. The challenge has always been to get delegates to own an idea when they might not be familiar with the concepts with which they are being trained. So I started to use isomorphic metaphors as a way of offering a solution. The delegates aren't aware that I'm doing this and therefore they take ownership of the ideas because they think they came up with them.

Here's an example in which I want delegates to come up with a way of challenging an objection. Specifically, I want them to have a way of getting a meeting with someone in a company when the person in that company says they don't have time for a meeting. My usual strategy is to turn the person's objection into a benefit for them. "Meeting me now means you save time in the long run." During the training session, if I just come out and say "Here's the strategy I want you to use", delegates don't own the idea even if they like it. But, if I use an isomorphic metaphor about ten minutes before I get onto the subject, I can covertly give them the strategy I want them to adopt. The information goes into their unconscious mind, waiting to be fired off. If I have to give them a nudge, all I have to do is make a link between the metaphor and getting the meeting. This fires off the strategy and the delegates own the idea. Everyone is happy.

Here's the metaphor I tell about ten minutes before I get to the content on securing meetings.

"A boy kept asking my daughter out when she was studying for exams but he couldn't understand why she wouldn't accept his advances. I liked the guy so eventually I said to him: 'If you want to meet someone who isn't that interested in meeting with you, you have to turn the reason they can't meet you into a benefit for them.' He was looking a little confused so I said: 'She doesn't have time to see you now because she's studying. If time is the thing she doesn't have a lot of, how can you make meeting you save her time?' Then I said: 'You're smart, you'll figure it out.' He thought for a moment and said: 'How about if I help her to study?' Bingo! My daughter got help with her studying, he got to see her and I got to keep an eye on both of them. Simple."

When I tell this type of metaphor, I'm usually delivering content and I just go into telling a story. I tend to tell quite a few stories in my training sessions, so no one really suspects anything. In fact, as I've told quite a few stories in this book, is it possible that some of them may have been pre-teaching information as well?

Anyway, here are some thoughts about this isomorphic metaphor. Firstly, notice how closely this metaphor mirrors the real life situation the delegates might find themselves in when trying to get a meeting with a client. All I have done is switch their challenge to a story about my daughter. Out of context, the metaphor just sounds like a story, especially with the line about keeping an eye on them at the end. When I contextualise it later on in the training session, by talking about the problem of getting a meeting, delegates are much more likely to come up with this as a solution themselves. Secondly, at certain points in the metaphor, and to make sure they get the message, I speak directly to the delegates. *If **you** want to meet someone who isn't that interested in meeting with **you**, **you** have to turn the reason they can't meet **you** into a benefit for them.* Then I give them an example of an actual problem they may encounter, the clients they want to see, but who don't have time for them. Then I tell them they are smart and will come up with an answer, which I want them to do in about ten minutes time.

How could you use this idea in your pitch? What kind of information might you want your clients to own as their own idea? How about your strategy? Or a payment structure? Or even part of your solution? You can choose anything. Now all you do is think up a metaphor that would interest your clients and embed your strategy into it.

There are a couple of other points about isomorphic metaphors that I need to cover before we move on.

One, keep the context of what you are doing out of their conscious awareness. You need to create a story that is far enough removed from the client's actual situation so that the metaphor remains a story for them. If they suspect anything, the barriers will go up and that will be that. One way to do this is to make your metaphor more abstract. In the beliefs section I talked about getting back from a foreign land as a way of symbolising the bringing of the client's global offices under one roof. Even this metaphor might be a little too obvious, but the good thing about it is that it's based on a real life event that actually happened for thousands of people and therefore could have happened to me.

Two, you could link your client's values statement to your metaphor. In the story about travelling back from Europe, I used the train to represent our company. By linking a client's values about getting back safely to the train, I'm creating a powerful unconscious link for the client. You already know how powerful values are, using a metaphor is just another way of linking them to your product or service.

Here's an isomorphic metaphor and I will leave you to discover its meaning. It shouldn't be too hard. Enjoy.

"A while back, a friend invited me to a fantastic event. The event was all about helping people and businesses grow and it came up with some really interesting and novel ways of tackling common business problems. This is exactly the kind of event I really love, so I was excited to go. I gained a lot of great information while I was there and really enjoyed myself. The next morning, after the event had finished, I went out to my car, which I had parked in a field. I got in and was about to back out, when I realised that the overnight rain had cause a mini lake behind me. I couldn't go back, because I would get stuck, which I couldn't afford to do. I looked at the cars parked in front of me and realised that it was the only way out. The gap looked worryingly narrow, so I started edging forward cautiously. I'll be honest, I wasn't sure if I could make it. I would stop and change direction, but only by enough to keep me moving forward. It took a little while to edge out, but finally I was free and I could get on with my journey."

Finally, and not specifically related to isomorphic metaphors. I suggest that you create a number of metaphors for yourself; that way you have lots of stories you can use when you need them. Some can be short and some long. Some could have a message and others designed to elicit emotions or provide solutions. I have a number of metaphors I use because I found people used to ask me the same questions again and again.

One of those questions was: "Marcus, how did you get into NLP?" I realised I could just tell the story, or I could tell a metaphor and include a lot of strategies, embedded commands and actions that I wanted them to take. I figured that if people were asking me this question, they might want to employ me. So I modified the original story, by a whisker, and the new story is what I tell people.

You've already read it. It's at the beginning of the book under the heading *opening the loop*, which is exactly what it did. It might be a good idea to go back and read it again; as you do, look out for the emotional states I'm taking you through, Pacing and Leading statements, language types, Emotional Impact words, the internal representations I'm forcing onto you, how I might be challenging your beliefs and feeding back values you might have given me. Or of course, you could just keep reading and let me tell you what and how I did what I did.

It was almost five years ago to the month, that my life changed (*set-up emotional hook: what changed my life? Starting to elicit curiosity*). I had gone with my family (*Emotional Impact word*), to stay with my parents for the weekend. They lived in a beautiful (*emotional language*) little cottage in the middle of a wheat field. There was nothing between us and the sea, apart from the wheat, which, as it was summer time, was ready for harvesting (*painting vivid pictures in the listeners mind*). I love (*emotion language*) the sea, and I used to walk with my children through the tracks in the field, down to the seawall, where we would scramble up the bank and onto the seawall (*lots of emotional words*). When you sit on the seawall, it's like there are so many opportunities, you can see (*visual language*) so many adventures unfolding in front of you, you can go anywhere, do anything (*switched from me to talking about you, lots of emotional language; drenching you in positive emotions about looking out to sea, set-up for later and being able to see opportunities – look at the internal representations I've created so far*). It's a great place to think, let your thoughts drift (*logical language and then, let your thoughts drift is a command*). Anyway, it was on this particular weekend, that everything changed (*engaging curiosity again, this is about state management and keeping the listener in the right emotional state*). Because I had taken my family (*Emotional Impact words*) home, my mum decided to have a tea party to introduce us to some other families, who were also up for the weekend. That Saturday afternoon two couples arrived for tea. I knew one of the couples, but not the other. After some pleasantries (*emotional language*), I found myself talking (*auditory language*) to the husband

I didn't know. I can't remember his name now, but we started talking, looking (*visual language*) for common ground, and I asked (*auditory language – hopefully by now you are getting the hang of the language types, so I'm going to point them out less*) him what he did. It turns out he's an architect working in the Far East. At that time I was a director, as in "lights, camera, action" and I was working with an architect who had a few projects in the Far East. Once I said I was a director, he wanted to know the kinds of things I was doing. I told him that I did commercials and high-end corporates. He said it sounded like a great job. (*I start to slow my speech down here*) I took a moment (*Pacing, I do when I tell the story*). I hadn't really thought that much about it before. And I certainly hadn't said it out loud (*Pacing*). But it wasn't. He looked at me (*Pacing, listener is looking at me*).

"Really," he said. "Why?"

I'm not sure exactly what happened next to make me say what I did; (*Pacing, I am going to say something*) it might have been the sea air or it could have been the fact that I didn't know this person at all (*Pacing, I don't necessarily know them*), but I felt like I could tell him what I really thought (*Pacing – I'm using lots of Pacing to make sure the listener is with me for what's coming*). So I just started talking (*Pacing*). And in that moment, I realised that I wasn't happy with where I had got to in my life. I wasn't producing the results I wanted to produce (*I'm starting to talk about something that everyone can really relate to, the universal theme of failing. I'm slowing right down now, drawing the listener in*). In fact, I felt like a failure. It was a pretty hard thing to admit (*Pacing*) but deep down I knew it was true. I had failed. And I had said it (*lots of emotional language, Emotional Impact words galore, failing, stuck. When I get to this bit in the story I slow right down so the listener can experience these emotions too. I'm using ambiguity so that the listener can think of times they have failed*). Then I realised just how stuck I really was (*starting to use words that imply I can't move*), because when you get into a spiral like that (*now I'm talking directly to the listener – you*), it's not easy to see a way out of it. The more you looked for answers, the more you realised you didn't have any (*again, I'm making it about you*). My stomach knotted the more I thought about it (*Pacing, this happens to most people and it might be happening for them now because I have directly involved them in the story – you*). At some point I remember looking up, into the face of the architect. He stood there with an expression that said, "I'm not a therapist and we're at a tea party" (*Pace, they probably weren't expecting this either*).

"Oh God, I'm so sorry, this really isn't anything to do with you. Really, I'm sorry..." (*Pace, I have actually said I'm sorry*) He looked at me, smiled and asked:

"If you're not producing the results you want, what are you going to do about it?" (*Lead, talking directly to the listener, it's a leading question that they have to think about answering.*) It was a pretty straightforward question, but my mind went completely blank (*Pace*) ...nothing (*Pace*) ...silence (*Pace*) ...it seemed to last for ages (*Pace, I do take ages to answer*) ...then three letters popped into my head. NLP (*super big Lead, this is the answer, and I'm starting to anchor them to me by tapping or pointing to my chest*). I had started to read a book on NLP and I had got about half way through and stopped, because 90% of the half I had read made no sense at all (*confusion pattern to embed the next sentence*). But I knew that was the answer (*anchor me again by tapping my chest*). So I told him how a friend of mine had met this amazing NLP trainer (*more anchoring me and it's a Pace because I'm telling the listener*) who had changed his life (*Pace*). So I decided that as soon as I got back, I was going to find out about this course (*Lead*). "That's how you produce different results," I said (*more anchoring me, lots of strategies I want people to do, get on course etc, with embedded commands. Also, Emotional Impact words and action words which brings them out of the feeling of being stuck and gives them a sense of movement towards where they want to go, plus it's a Lead*). And I did! The course was brilliant. Which is why I'm here now telling you about it (*Pace, I am telling them*). You see I realised two things during the training, which changed my life completely (*emotional hook again, more state management, offering them hope. Words like brilliant, offer, hope, force powerful images into their mind about*

NLP and training). The first was, if you always do what you've always done, you will always produce the same results (*Pace, it's true*). So if you're happy with the results you're producing right now, you don't need to do anything different, it's simple (*this is a direct question to the listener – no one is ever producing the results they want, therefore set up for the next line*). But if you're not, you have to try something new (*Lead*).

The second thing, well that's the biggie (*hook, firing off curiosity*). That's the thing that changed everything forever (*emotional hook*). Am I glad I went on that course? Of course I am. I believe that if you want to be the best you can be, you have to do something you love, then you're driven to succeed (*these are all pacing statements*). I can see where I'm going again. That's why I'll keep doing it... (*Lead and breaking the story off without concluding it so I can start to deliver the content, visual language, lots of Emotional Impact words, lots of positive internal pictures*).

And that's it. Of course I'm going to conclude the metaphor (close the loop), because I have left you hanging, not knowing what the "biggie" is. I just have to deliver all my content first.

Metaphors in pictures

A picture paints a thousand words. Now, there's a metaphor and in this section it's a nice introduction to what we're going to be looking at. Pictures and pitches go hand in hand. Pictures create emotions within us, in the same way that Emotional Impact words do. A father holding a baby fires off strong emotions that would take time to convey with words.

Most people use some kind of pictures in their pitch, even if it's only in the background or a picture of the client's product. There are a couple of ideas I want to explore in this section, that can help you use pictures more persuasively.

Firstly, as I said, pictures help to get across ideas much faster than words. They are often more engaging than listening to a nervous presenter. Therefore make use of them. Don't shy away from using pictures, but do shy away from using pictures that don't help you. Think about the emotions your pictures will fire off in your client.

An image with a meaning, that isn't immediately obvious, is a powerful way of engaging with your client, because they will be looking for ways to interpret that image to make it relevant to what you're saying. There are two reasons why you might want this to happen. Firstly, and to spell it out, you will be engaging your client's curiosity again. This is another covert way of creating this desired emotional state during your pitch. Secondly, if your client works out the meaning of the image before you tell them, they will congratulate themselves, it's the "Aha, I get it!" moment. Even if they get the relationship between the image and what you are saying as you're saying it, they will still have that "Aha!" moment. So now you have added the feeling of intelligence to their curiosity.

Another thing you can do in your pitch is string a set of visual metaphors together to create a visual theme. This is useful if you want to create a link between your visual theme and something that you want your client to see as related – even if it is apparently unrelated. It's like Pacing and Leading with images. A simple example, and the easiest way to do this, is to choose a theme in your pitch, say growth. Every time you talk about growth or have a slide about growth, you use a specific colour on that slide. Your clients will start to associate that colour with growth. Once you have the theme established, you can link your growth colour to anything you want your clients to see as an opportunity for growth, even when it may not be. Here's an example:

1. Talk about growth. Accompanying slide has a green background.
2. Talk about growth. Accompanying slide has a green background.
3. Talk about growth. Accompanying slide has a green background.
4. Talk about growth. Accompanying slide has a green background.

5. Talk about moving your client's business to your company. Accompanying slide has a green background.

By talking about moving your client's business to you, you fire off an unconscious response associated with growth. You can use this idea with any theme in your pitch, as long as you have spent enough time setting up the link between what you talk about and the colour associated with it. I would recommend that you set up the link at least four times. Obviously, the subtler the colour you use, the more unconscious the link is, which makes what you're doing less obvious.

As well as doing this with colours, you can also do it with boxes in your slides. I'm going to talk about two box shapes, regular square boxes and boxes with rounded edges. These boxes can be boxes that contain information like numbers, or boxes that frame the entire slide. Anywhere where you talk about concrete facts, information that the client has supplied you or information that your client knows as a fact, use regular square boxes. This sets up a theme, square boxes = facts. Anywhere where you use information that isn't an absolute fact, you can use boxes with rounded edges. When you want information to be perceived as an absolute fact, even when it isn't, use a regular square box.

The final way you could use this idea, is to use a set of visual metaphors. If we take growth again, an obvious example of growth is trees, especially if your client is environmentally friendly. Visual images you could use are: trees, leaves, seeds, roots, sunlight, watering, soil, planting, spring, summer, new shoots and so on. Select four or more images from your list and use these images in your slides when you are talking about how you are going to help your client grow their own business. You have now started a visual set. Again, once you have the theme established, you can link your growth theme to a slide where you want your clients to see a point you're making as an opportunity for growth, even when it isn't.

There are a couple of slides you might want to have in your pitch because they convey important metaphors. A welcome slide. Make it relevant to your client. Have an image that sets up the journey you are going to take them on during the pitch. Your image also wants to fire off positive emotions for your client. Bearing this in mind, I was thinking about a welcome slide for a fashion brand pitch. The image I had in mind was of an empty catwalk with people sitting around the sides waiting expectantly. I thought this would conjure up the emotions of excitement and anticipation as well as being an image the client could relate to. Then it was pointed out that fashion shows are very stressful places and that I might fire off a negative set of emotions for the client instead of the positive emotions I wanted. It's not surprising then that we didn't use my welcome slide idea! The other slide I'm going to recommend you use is a slide that says the pitch is over but the journey together is just beginning. Think about a slide you could use that would deliver that message visually.

Summary

- Metaphors are a powerful way of communicating.
- You can create metaphors that elicit emotions, contain a hidden messages or that offer a solution to a problem faced by your client.
- To create an emotional metaphor, you need to think of what emotion you want to elicit in your client. Then think of a time when you felt that emotion and only that emotion. Get as much detail back from that time as possible. Really bring it to life. This will have an impact on your non-verbal communication.
- When you recount this metaphor, get into the emotional state first.
- Bring the metaphor to life using language types.
- End the metaphor as you are building to the peak of the state you want to elicit, about 80-90% into your metaphor.
- As soon as you have elicited the emotional state you want, start delivering your content. At the end of your content, conclude the last part of your metaphor.

- Metaphors that contain a hidden message bypass conscious resistance.

- Use **Incident, Point, Benefit** to create your metaphor and hidden message.

- Your hidden message is more likely to be acted upon if it contains a benefit your client is interested in.

- Wrap your metaphor in something your client is interested in.

- Isomorphic metaphors offer your clients a solution to a problem or challenge they're currently facing.

- To create an isomorphic metaphor, you need to mirror your client's real life situation.

- As you talk about their situation in your metaphor, you can offer up a solution for them.

- Isomorphic metaphors are also a good way to help your clients take ownership of an idea.

- Create a number of different stories you can use as and when you need to.

- You can embed powerful strategies and learning, messages and commands in a metaphor.

- Picture metaphors are useful way of firing off emotional states.

- You can create a theme by repeating the same type of pictures, colours or boxes in your presentation.

- Once you have established your theme, you can link it to something that isn't related. You can establish a growth theme and then link it to something that is unrelated to growth.

- It will help you if your first and last slides are metaphors that set up the journey you're about to take your clients on.

Exercises

- Think about what emotional state you want to elicit in your clients during your pitch and create a metaphor around this state. Practise and then deliver it to your colleagues in your rehearsals.
- Think about the questions you normally get asked when you first meet someone or when you interact with a client. Create three **Incident, Point, Benefit** metaphors with hidden messages that you could use in these circumstances.
- What challenges are your clients facing?
- Create an isomorphic metaphor that mirrors their challenges and offers a solution.
- Come up with some ideas to create visual themes in your pitch. Start with something easy, like using different types of boxes. See what happens when you do this. Try it out on your colleagues, see if they notice what you have done.

As we're about half way through Part Three of this book, I want you to rate how much more persuasive you believe you could be in your next pitch as a result of the information you now have. Please write your percentage improvement score below.

	%

4.
THE EXTRA 10%

How to use your client's colours more persuasively in your pitch

I'M NOT GOING TO TALK about what colours mean in this section, just how you can incorporate your client's corporate colour palette into your pitch, in a way that will help you to be more persuasive. Your clients spend a lot of money getting their corporate colours and logo right. Even in big organisations, people care about the company colours, logo and what they represent to themselves and the world. They'll therefore respond to these colours in a positive way. You are going to use your client's inbuilt emotional response to their company colour palette to help them connect more powerfully to your ideas, products, services or figures (savings, ROI) during your pitch.

There are a number of ways you could do this. Firstly, you could incorporate your client's colour palette slowly into your presentation. At the beginning of your presentation, use your normal colours. Hopefully, they will be colours that make up part of your own company's colour palette. As you start to talk more about solutions and how you can help your clients, subtly start to incorporate more of their colours into your slides. This technique creates a powerful unconscious relationship between you and your client. By the end of your presentation, both companies' colour palettes should be used. If you can only use one or two of your client's colours don't worry, it will be better than nothing. For this technique to be really effective, you have to keep the introduction of their company colours out of their conscious awareness. You don't want them to sit there and suddenly think: "Hello, what's going on here? Why have they suddenly started to use our colours?"

Another idea is to incorporate your client's colours into your benefits slides. As an example, you can use one of your client's colours for your projected ROI figures, or other figures your client is interested in.

Year 1	Year 2	Year 3	Total Growth from Year 1
200 units	320 units	430 units	230 units

The "230 units" is in one of your client's colours. If you want to be really subtle about this, use a colour that's close to one you are already using in this slide, or you could graduate the colours in the line until you end up with the client's own. Alternatively you could highlight a row of beneficial figures on a slide in one of your client's colours.

There are lots of ways you could apply your client's colour palette to your presentation. Try different ideas out and have fun when creating your next pitch, it's likely to rub off on the way you design and present your ideas.

Summary

- Clients are emotionally attached to their corporate colours.
- You can use your client's corporate colours to fire off their emotions.
- You can use your client's corporate colour pallet by including it in your presentation.
- You can slowly introduce their colour pallet into your slides, conveying that you are coming together.
- You can use specific colours to highlight benefits with which you want them to associate.

Exercises

- Find out your client's corporate colour pallet and find a way to subtly incorporate it into your presentation.

How to anchor positive emotions about you and your product, in your client's future

Imagine if you could fire off positive emotions about you, your product, service or company, and associate these emotions with something happening in your client's future.

Well you can and the good news is that it's not as difficult as it first sounds.

We all have a way of encoding time in our minds. For most people when they think about their future, it's either in front of them or to their right. When we think about our past, it is either behind us or to the left of us.

During your pitch, it's possible to mark out the area you occupy when you are presenting, so that it represents the past and the future for your clients. When your clients are facing you, their right is associated with their future and their left with the past. So these are the areas you want to mark out for them. To do this, every time you talk about the future (which you do a lot in a pitch), stand in an area to the right of your clients, and talk about their future. To mark out their past, you stand in an area to their left, and talk about what has happened. See diagram below. If you do this every time you talk about their past or future, you will quickly build up an unconscious association for your clients in these two areas. This process is known as spatial anchoring. If you want to talk to them about something that is happening for them in the present, you stand in the middle of your presenting area (the "now" area).

Clients

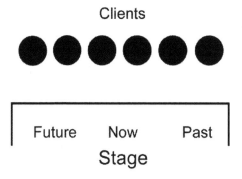

Everybody presenting information in your pitch has to stand in the correct area when they are talking about the same *past*, *present* or *future*, for this to work effectively. Once you have established these areas in your client's minds, you can then start to talk about bad things or problems in the past area, and positive things in the future area. ROI, successes, savings, testimonials, or any information that will make your client feel good, stand in the future area. This is how you anchor positive emotions about you and your product or service into your client's future. Similarly, you can dump unwanted or negative emotions and problems in the past by moving over to that area and dealing with them there. This way, unconsciously, it will be seen as being something in the past.

Just to be clear, your client's future is on their right, as they're looking at you. Therefore it's on your left. This will be counter-intuitive for many people. If you start walking to your right to anchor positive emotions, you are walking into your clients past. I once saw a presenter who kept walking into my past when he was talking about my future, it's confusing but I didn't understand why. It was as though there was something not quite right about what he was saying but I couldn't put my finger on it. You need to avoid this kind of confusion during your pitch.

Summary

- You can anchor positive emotions into your client's future by marking out part of the area in which you present. You do this by talking about their future and standing to the right of your clients.
- Similarly you can mark out the past for your clients by talking about the past when you stand to their left.
- To utilize this concept, establish the Future and Past area, then talk about success and benefits in their future.
- Dump problems and challenges into the past area.

Exercises

- When you rehearse, use tape to represent the Past and Future areas in your pitch.
- Actually get your presenter to physically move between the two areas, depending on what they are talking about.

How to get the questions you
want at the end of your pitch

You made it all the way through your pitch and it went well. Now you have the questions. How many times have you wished you didn't have to take any questions at all? How many times have you felt that the questions are the one bit you couldn't really prepare for? I mean, they could ask anything, right? The sky's the limit!

What if your clients didn't ask you just anything? What if you could find a way to get your clients to ask more of the questions you wanted them to ask? Why chance getting asked something you don't want to answer, or worse still, could make you look bad?

So how could you control the questions you get asked? It's actually pretty simple, but it does rely on you doing one thing. It relies on you using the *4MAT System*. You see if you use the *4MAT System* all the way through your pitch, your audience will become accustomed to having the information delivered to them in that order, which is how you get them to ask the questions you want at the end of the pitch.

Simple, right?

Are you reading this thinking that something is missing? That I haven't explained it all? Do you have a question? Is that question, **How** do you use the *4MAT System* to get the questions you want? Then you have just answered the question of how you get your clients to ask the questions you want at the end of your pitch. You leave out, or only give an overview of, part of the **How**. It's the one piece of information that everyone will want to know, especially, if it's an important point.

The opposite is also true. If you want to avoid questions on a section of your pitch, in that section give lots of detail about how you're going to achieve the result. Answer all the questions your client might come up with before they are actually asked. If you give a detailed, step-by-step breakdown that outlines everything they would need to know, what questions could they ask? I once heard a great way to win a debate, which is based upon a similar principle. If you go first, stand up and argue the other side's case, as if you were arguing it for them. You talk about everything they would talk about. Then one by one, you point out why each point doesn't work. Then you sit down again. This doesn't leave the other side with anything to talk about.

How to answer questions that have a negative impact on your clients

The answers to questions asked at the end of the pitch fall into two emotional categories. Firstly, there are answers that make your client feel good about themselves. Then there are answers which might challenge your client or fire off a negative emotion for them.

Having got all the way through your pitch, it would be a shame to fall at the last hurdle. So I'm going to share with you an idea on how to deal with questions where the client may not like the answers.

The simplest way to do this is to use an isomorphic metaphor. You still talk about the challenge or concern, but instead of answering the question directly you are going to talk about something you have done, or something that you have done for one of your other clients.

In my training sessions, if I get asked a question that would make the delegate look bad, I don't just come out with that answer. Instead, I prefer to tell a story about something I did which mirrors their situation very closely. I tend to make it self-deprecating and funny if I can. At the end of the story, I tell them what I did to get around the problem. By answering a tricky question this way, I'm not making any of the delegates look bad or feel stupid and I'm giving them the information they need, in a way that keeps them in a positive emotional state.

Of course, I know the kinds of questions I'm going to get asked, so I have a number of stories to hand. If you get caught and you can't answer a question using a metaphor, my advice is, thank the client for the question, and try to frame it as positively as possible.

Summary

- You can use the *4MAT System* to help you get the questions you want at the end of your pitch.
- Leaving out or only giving an overview of the How is usually enough to get your clients wanting to know more.
- Similarly, if you want to reduce the number of questions about a section of your pitch, give lots of detail in the *Why, What, How* and *What if.*
- When you answer questions that might frustrate your client or make them look bad, try an isomorphic metaphor. This way they get the information they need, without the negative emotion.

Exercises

- Try leaving out some of your *How* in a meeting with a client and see what happens.
- Then try it in a pitch.
- Think about what questions you might get asked at the end of your pitch. What questions could annoy, frustrate or make your client look bad? Think of some isomorphic metaphors you could use to make your point and keep your clients in a positive emotional state.

As we come to the end of book, please write in a percentage improvement score for how much more persuasive you believe you could be in your next pitch as a result of all the information you now possess.

	%

CLOSING THE LOOP

...BECAUSE I LOVE IT! And the biggie? The most important lesson? That you really can have what you want. Of course you have to work at it. You have to study, that's a given. And I studied and studied. I read books, listened to audio programmes, watched videos and I went on courses, lots of courses, so that I would have the very best skills and knowledge available. I learnt from the best of the best, so I could start to produce the same results as them and be the best I could be. The more I learnt, the more I started to believe in myself, in what I could do and slowly I started to act in accordance with these new beliefs. I changed the way I did things and that's when my results changed.

And you know, some days, it's like walking through that wheat field, on a beautiful sunny, summer's day, feeling the sun on your back. The journey is always worth it. It's always great. And as you walk towards the seawall, a funny thing seems to happen. The closer you get, the less daunting it looks. It's never quite as big as you think it's going to be. So you scramble up the bank, to the top and when you get up there, when you're standing on the seawall, there's nothing like it. The view is amazing. You can see for miles and miles. I love the sea because you can go anywhere, that's what I really love about being up there. The possibilities. It's like the world has no limits when you're there. You can feel the sun on your back and the warm summer breeze on your face. But most of all, you can see all the opportunities opening up in front of you. And you know, there are seats up there, in fact there are lots of seats up there, and I bet, if you were to look, you would find one with your name on it. It's there, I promise you that; it's waiting for you.

ABOUT THE AUTHOR

NLP SEEMS TO BE EVERYWHERE NOW. That's for a very good reason – it's a powerful set of techniques that allow anyone to create the most effective and impactful communication possible.

For many people, the basics of NLP are something they do quite naturally, with no real understanding of how they are so good at what they do.

Marcus is one of those people. Before becoming an NLP trainer, Marcus, had been pitching for business for over 15 years as a commercials and corporate film director. In this competitive environment, he worked with global brands like: Toyota, Cisco Systems, British Airways, Ford, Channel 4, IBM and many others.

After extensive training, Marcus realised he could use NLP more formally to replicate his results for others.

Marcus is a sought-after NLP Master Practitioner and trainer, now working as a consultant and coach with a proven track record in helping companies maximise their own pitch conversion ratios and sales results.

Marcus currently works in sectors as diverse as financial services, retail, property development, internet services, recruitment and with some of the world's leading communications agencies. His unique interpretation of the latest NLP thinking offers organizations a cutting edge solution that's grounded in real world advice, producing fast, practical results that can be easily tailored to any existing new business strategy.

Learn more at: *www.marcuscorah.com*

BONUS PAGE

Dear reader,

I would like to invite you to learn more about winning business, by offering you an opportunity to download my free audio programme on profiling your clients during your pre-pitch meetings.

This programme will show you the key things to look out for to determine your client's personality type and then suggest the language you could use to influence or motivate them.

You can download my audio programme right now at: *www.marcuscorah.com/bonus2461.html*

REFERENCE NOTES

Part Two, Chapter 1. Designing persuasive content
1. McCarthy, Bernice. Used with special permission.
2. Ledochowski, Igor & Mee, Clifford *The Power of Conversational Hypnosis*. Page 35

Part Three, Chapter 1. *Advanced language ideas*
1. Ledochowski, Igor & Mee, Clifford *The Power of Conversational Hypnosis*. Page 210

COURSES AND DOWNLOADS

The Quest Institute. *Practitioner and Master Practitioner courses in NLP and Cognitive hypnotherapy practitioner training.*

Christopher Howard Training. *NLP Trainers Training and Advanced Presenter Immersion.*

Igor Ledochowski & Clifford Mee. *The Power of Conversational Hypnosis.* Online course.

Rintu Basu. *Advanced Persuasion Patterns.* Online course.

BIBLIOGRAPHY

Bandler, Richard & La Valle, John, *Persuasion Engineering*, Meta Publications, 1996

Bandler, Richard & Grinder, John, *Patterns of the Hypnotic Techniques of Milton H. Erickson, M.D Volume 1*, Meta Publications, 1975

Basu, Rintu, *Persuasion Skills Black Book: Practical NLP Language Patterns for Getting The Response You Want*, Bookshaker, 2009

Cialdini, Robert, *Influence: The Psychology of Persuasion*, Harper Collins College Publishers, 1993

James, Tad & Shephard, David, *Presenting Magically: Transforming Your Stage Presence With NLP*, Crown House Publishing, 2001

Printed by Amazon Italia Logistica S.r.l.
Torrazza Piemonte (TO), Italy